WINNING FOOTBALL WITH THE OPTION PACKAGE OFFENSE

Bob Petrino with Marty Mouat

Parker Publishing Company
West Nyack, N.Y.

© 1986 by

PARKER PUBLISHING COMPANY, INC.
West Nyack, N.Y.

10 9 8 7 6 5 4 3 2

Library of Congress Cataloging-in-Publication Data
Petrino, Bob, 1937–
    Winning football with the option package offense.
    Includes index.
    1. Football—Offense. 2. Football—Coaching.
I. Mouat, Marty, 1947–   . II. Title.
GV951.8.P47 1985   796.33212   85-21420

ISBN 0-13-960931-8

Printed in the United States of America

ABOUT THE AUTHOR

Bob Petrino is head football coach at Carroll College in Helena, Montana. In twenty-five years of coaching at the high school and collegiate level, he has guided sixteen championship teams. Petrino's overall record is 135-57-1.

In thirteen years at Carroll, Petrino has coached the Fighting Saints to eight Frontier Conference championships, two undefeated regular seasons, and an NAIA playoff game. He has been named Frontier Conference Football Coach of the Year six times and NAIA District 12 (Montana, North Dakota, and South Dakota) Coach of the Year once.

Under Petrino's leadership, Carroll has ranked in the top twenty in NAIA Division II final rankings three times.

CONTENTS

HOW YOU WILL SUCCEED WITH THE OPTION PACKAGE OFFENSE

At Carroll College, we face personnel problems similar to those faced by most high school teams. We offer no full scholarships for football. Therefore, we are not able to "out-man" our opponents on a regular basis.

Yet, we consistently have been a successful offensive team. And we have moved the ball because our option package offense is sound. This offense is not merely a series of plays. It is a flexible system of action and reaction. If the defense does one thing, we will adjust with something else. Because we have moved the ball, we have been able to win eight conference championships in thirteen years, go undefeated twice in regular season play, and receive an NAIA playoff bid.

Why don't we have to "out-man" our opponents every game? Because if we cannot block the line of scrimmage with our "I" formation offense, we will use our finesse offense, our veer offense. In the veer, plays develop quickly. There is much double-team or good angle blocking. Many times we read on a defense man instead of blocking him.

Our offense utilizes the best of two systems. The "I" is a ball-control offense. It is used for power play inside and the sprint-out passing game to the outside. The counter and inside series from the "I" are also effective.

The veer is a big play offense. Our veer offense includes the inside and outside veer, counter, counter option, lead option, loaded option, and crazy option.

No offense is complete without an effective passing game. Our option package offense includes three passing games—the sprint-out game, the play action game, and the explosive quick-passing game.

Some coaches do not believe that you can coach two different offenses. Our staff's answer is that you can teach a football player many different principles if your teaching process is sound. This book will show you exactly what our teaching process is and how your offense can include both the power game of the "I" and the finesse, "big play" game of the veer.

Our option package offense has been successful for us and it has remained successful for us. While we have always been an option team, our offense is not the same as it was ten years ago, or even one year ago.

There are two reasons for adapting an offense. First, defensive coaches are forever adjusting. If offensive coaches don't also adjust, their teams will be unable to move the ball. Two examples of ways in which we adapt our offense to defensive adjustments are misdirection and the quick-passing game.

The second reason a coach must adapt offensively is because his personnel changes yearly. We have emphasized the "I" formation in the years we have had a big offensive line and a strong running back. When we have been smaller in the offensive line, we have leaned more to the veer.

Thus, our option package offense has evolved and adjusted, both to defensive changes and to our own personnel changes. This offense can successfully attack any defensive set or coverage as long as it is executed properly.

Chapter 1 discusses the option package offense, while Chapter 2 deals with the selection and adaption of personnel. Our alignments, formations, and numbering system are among the subjects discussed in Chapter 3. Our blocking system is covered in Chapter 4.

Chapter 5, "Coaching the 'I' Formation Running Game," includes philosophy and execution of all plays. Chapter 6 discusses "Developing the Triple Option from the 'I' and Veer." Chapter 7 shows how we teach the veer offense.

Chapter 8, "Incorporating the Option Package Passing Game," covers philosophy and execution of the sprint-out, play-action, and quick-passing games. Chapter 9 covers "Coaching the Split Receivers."

Chapter 10, "Training the Option Quarterback," includes the reading of defenses and an effective automatic system.

Chapter 11, "Implementing an Effective Team Offense," discusses seven effective team offensive drills.

The little things that make the difference between winning and losing are covered in Chapter 12, "Developing the Winning Edge."

Chapter 13 shows why building an offense is a year-round job.

You are invited to read on to victory. Remember, you must score to win.

1

THE OPTION

PACKAGE OFFENSE

The option package offense includes:

1. The triple option or inside veer
2. The outside veer
3. The loaded option
4. The pass-first, run-second option
5. The trap option
6. The counter option
7. The windback
8. The counter dive
9. The fullback trap

All of these plays are run from split backs. The inside veer, trap option, windback, and fullback trap are also run from the "I" formation.

THE TRIPLE OPTION OR INSIDE VEER

The triple option or inside veer is a good play if you are facing bigger people. The inside veer will give you a way to out-finesse teams since you are not relying on man blocking.

You want to do three things with the inside veer. First, you want to create blocking angles to seal inside.

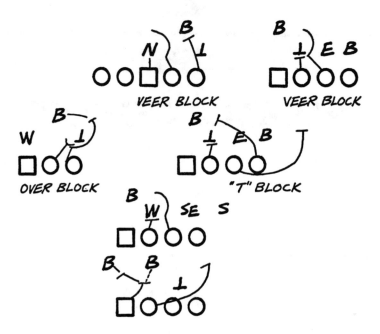

Second, you are trying to out-finesse two people to the outside.

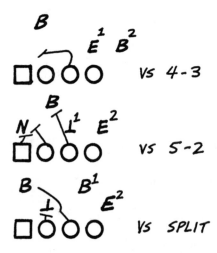

Third, you are trying to get the football to one of three alleys. The first alley is from the inside of the offensive tackle's leg to the difference between the tackle and the slot back. The second alley is from the difference between the tackle and slot back to the difference between the slot back and split end. The slot back and split end line up nine yards apart. The third alley is from the difference between the slot back and split end to the sideline.

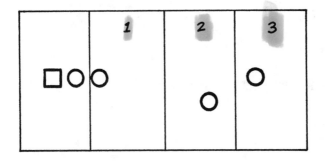

THE OUTSIDE VEER

The outside veer is designed to give a three-on-two situation with a read. You can show the defense a formation and then force the defense into a three-on-two situation by changing the formation. The outside veer is an outstanding play in short-yardage and goal-line situations.

Outside veer versus 5-2 defense:

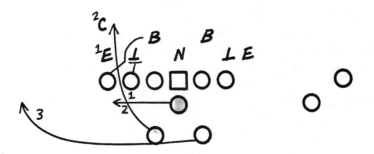

Outside veer versus 4-3 defense:

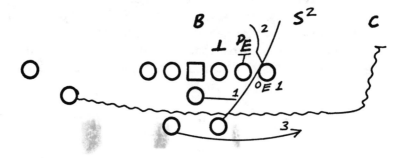

Outside veer versus a split defense:

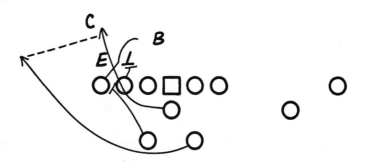

LOADED OPTION

There are two reasons for using the loaded option. First, it takes advantage of a quarterback who has excellent quickness and speed. Second, it allows the pitch upfield.

In the loaded option, you are blocking the first read. The quarterback must read the running back's block. If the running back blocks the defensive end inside out, the quarterback should turn upfield. If the running back hooks the defensive end, the quarterback must step around the block.

Loaded option versus a 5-2 defense:

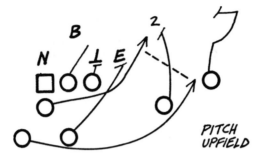

PASS-FIRST, RUN-SECOND OPTION

The pass-first, run-second option is part of the option package offense for three reasons. First, it takes advantage of secondary backs coming fast to the alleys to stop the option.

Second, it can result in a big play or a touchdown. Third, after the pass-first, run-second option is successful, defensive backs are forced to stop coming hard to the alleys. This makes it easier to pitch the ball.

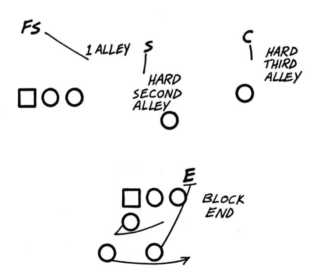

The defense will be unable to rotate quickly to all three alleys. The quarterback reads the cornerback. The split end also reads the corner. If the corner rolls, the split end runs the two route.
Split end running the two route:

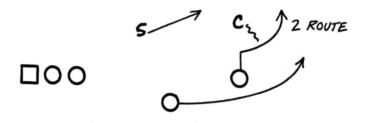

If the corner rotates to ⅓ deep, the split end runs the 1 route. Split end running the one route:

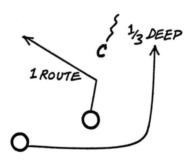

This is just one example of the pass-first, run-second option. In our system, the routes are called 81 and 82 read.

TRAP OPTION

There are four reasons why the trap option is an important part of the option package offense.

First, the trap option gives misdirection and allows you to seal inside more effectively.

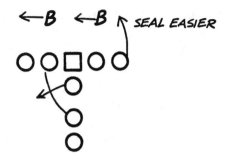

Second, it allows you to get the ball to the pitch man. The defensive end comes hard. The guard hits the defensive end inside and forearm blocks "two." "Two" could be the corner or the safety, depending on the formation.

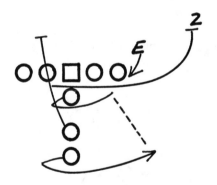

Third, the trap option gives you a way to protect your quarterback. The guard's block protects the quarterback. With a hard defensive end, the hit gives the quarterback time to pitch.

Fourth, the trap option allows you to pitch the ball upfield. With a soft defensive end, the guard blocks inside out so the pitch man can get inside.

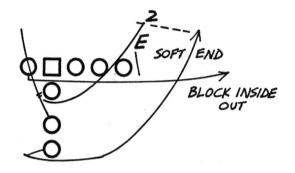

COUNTER OPTION

The Counter Option does three things. First, it gives misdirection. The quarterback starts in one direction and then comes back.

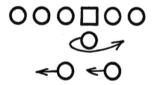

Second, it allows you to seal inside more effectively.

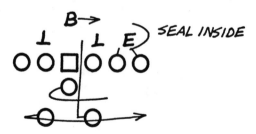

Third, the Counter Option stops quick pursuit against the triple option because the defense is forced to read the counter option. The Counter Option is an excellent play against quick-pursuit teams.

THE WINDBACK, COUNTER DIVE, AND FULLBACK TRAP

These three plays are designed to attack the middle with misdirection. They will keep the defense honest in the middle and force the defense to keep its linebackers at home.

The windback looks like the option in its initial phase.

The Windback:

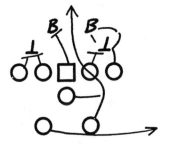

The Counter Dive:

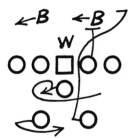

The Fullback Trap:

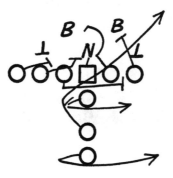

MOTION

There is something else that is essential to the option package offense—motion.

First, you want to run motion away from the defensive strength, make the defense adjust to the motion, and then attack the defensive weakness. Second, you want to create an alley. Third, when the defense replaces the alley, you may be able to get a big play with the pass.

In conclusion, the entire option package—the Triple Option or Inside Veer; the Outside Veer; the Loaded Option; the Pass-First, Run-Second Option; the Trap Option; the Counter Option; the Windback; the Counter Dive; and the Fullback Trap—must be run in order to attack all of the opposition's defensive looks and adjustments.

2

USING PERSONNEL TO
MAXIMUM ADVANTAGE

Without the right kind of players, the best offensive system in the world will not be consistently effective. Therefore, a coach's first task is to select "his" kind of players. Then, he must fit those players into the positions where they can be the most effective.

This chapter will discuss the kind of people we try to recruit for our football program at Carroll College. Your personnel requirements may be quite different.

But regardless of individual requirements, there are several principles that remain constant. First, you don't always need the greatest physical talent to be successful. However, you must have players with enough basic intelligence to understand your system, "winners" who will pay the price on the practice field and in the weight room and players who can execute.

Some years you will have more talent than other years. But even great talent will not be a guarantee of success if your players don't understand your system, don't pay the price to be "winners," and don't execute consistently.

We will also discuss how we fit our personnel into individual offensive positions. Once again, your individual requirements may vary greatly, but the principles remain the same.

We will conclude the chapter by elaborating on three main points. First, we will consider the relationship between execution and sound habit formation. Second, we will explain how a coach must take advantage of what his players can do. Third, we will show why a coach must understand his players' limitations.

THE OFFENSIVE LINE

The offensive line is the second most difficult place to play in football next to the defensive secondary. A team's offense is only as good as its offensive line.

Therefore, we place great emphasis on the selection of our offensive linemen.

There are several things we look for in an offensive lineman. First, we would like all of our linemen to have a tall frame. We always try to put fifteen to twenty pounds on our offensive linemen if they have the growth potential. The taller a player is, the more growth potential he has.

However, we often must settle for smaller linemen.

The other attributes we look for in an offensive lineman are upper body strength, quick feet, "heart," and technique.

Once an offensive lineman gets to Carroll, the order changes a little. The first thing we work on is a player's technique. We are very much a technique offensive-line football team. Our philosophy is that technique is perfected only through continuous repetition.

We also try to build upper body strength in our linemen. The minimum our offensive linemen should be able to bench press is 300 pounds.

It is not enough that our offensive linemen have good technique and upper body strength. They should also have quick feet. Our quickness excercises include jumping benches, "ups and downs," and jumping rope. We want our linemen to be able to jump rope as many times in a minute as their weight. This is harder for most of them to accomplish than the 300-pound bench press.

We also give our offensive linemen considerable work on squats with the squat machine and the leaper machine. Squats will improve our players' quickness off the ball as well as their 40-yard dash times. We continually stress getting off the ball quickly and spend ten minutes every practice on get-off drills.

If an offensive lineman has intelligence, growth potential, upper body strength, quick feet, and explosiveness off the ball, he may still not be the kind of player we are looking for. Why? Because, we also want players who have "heart."

To us, "heart" is second effort and third effort. One way to judge "heart" is to watch what a lineman does away from the ball. Usually, when an offensive lineman has a play run to his side, he will be giving the best effort he can. We want the player who gives the same kind of effort when the play is run to the other side.

"Heart" can also be determined by what an offensive lineman does after the initial block. We have had a lineman make three blocks on one play.

Something else worth watching is what a player does when he misses a block. Does he get back up and still try to make a play? If he does, he probably has the kind of "heart" we are looking for.

Thus, the general attributes we look for in our offensive linemen are intelligence, growth potential, upper body strength, quick feet, explosiveness off the ball, "heart," and proper technique.

There are also some specific position attributes we look for.

TIGHT END

Ideally, our tight end would be about 6'4" tall and weigh 230 pounds. The first thing we judge a tight end on is his blocking ability. Then we judge him on his ability to catch the football. Our tight end must be able to help block on the offensive tackle hole and his position requires quick feet.

QUICK TACKLE

We flip-flop our offensive line by moving our linemen from one side of the line to the other depending on the play. Our quick tackle and quick guard always line up next to each other whether it be to the right or left of our center. Likewise, our strong guard, strong tackle, and tight end are always next to each other.

We want our most experienced offensive tackle at quick tackle because he must do a lot of one-on-one blocking.

The ideal height and weight for our quick tackle would be 6'4" and 240 pounds. We also want him to have good quick feet. But again, you don't always get what you want. Many years we have played with smaller tackles.

QUICK GUARD

We also put our most experienced guard at the quick guard spot. We trap a lot with our quick guard, and he does a great deal of one-on-one blocking. He must also be able to execute what we call our slide block.

Ideally, our quick guard would weigh 230 to 240 pounds but we have many times played with a smaller athlete. Our quick guard must again have good quick feet and good upper body strength.

STRONG TACKLE AND STRONG GUARD

Our strong tackle and strong guard are usually in the same size, strength, and quickness range as our quick tackle and quick guard. However, the strong tackle and strong guard are usually less experienced. Most of our guards and tackles start on the strong side, where they can do more double-team blocking. By the time they are juniors or seniors, those guards and tackles are lining up on the quick side.

There is a matter of pride here. If a player begins his career on the strong side, he *expects* to be on the quick side before his playing days are over.

CENTER

Most of the time, our centers have been small people with quick feet and good upper body strength.

Center is the position we generally reserve for a person who really wants to play the game. This is a position for a real "winner" who has to play somewhere. He may not have the size, but he has paid the price in the weight room and on the practice field.

WIDE RECEIVERS

We would like our split end to be a lanky athlete who can run and jump. He should have good hands, mental toughness, and discipline. Some years we have been fortunate to have split ends who could run the 40-yard dash in 4.6 seconds. Other years we have had to get by with 4.7 or 4.75 players.

We would also like our split end to have a vertical jump of thirty to thirty-two inches, though many years we have fielded players who had lesser vertical jumps.

We like our slot backs to have the same abilities as our split ends—some speed, good hands, and jumping ability. We would also like our slot back to be a little more physical type of player with some upper body strength. This is because he must be able to execute the crack-back block and the control block.

All of our receivers must have mental toughness and mental discipline. They must also be able to read all secondary coverages.

We realize we won't usually get receivers with blazing speed. They are going to attend schools where they can get full scholarships. Therefore, we must do a good job of teaching technique. We must "out-execute" the defensive secondary.

QUARTERBACK

The most important attribute a quarterback can have is leadership ability. He must be a "winner" type.

Next, he must be a good athlete—a good basketball player, a good golfer, etc. We like our quarterbacks to play golf because it is a sport that demands great concentration. You must concentrate to hit the golf ball and you must also concentrate to be a sound quarterback.

We want quarterbacks with quick feet and a quick passing release. We don't want quarterbacks who wind up slowly to throw.

As for speed, we have had quarterbacks who were no faster than 5.1 seconds in the 40-yard dash all the way down to 4.6. A big selling point for our option package offense is that we have moved the ball with quarterbacks of varying physical abilities.

But one thing all of our quarterbacks must have, regardless of individual physical characteristics, is intelligence. They must understand the defenses they are seeing, change plays, read areas in the line, and read areas in the secondary.

RUNNING BACK

A running back should have good body balance. Our offense is designed to get our backs into one-on-one situations with the defenders, so we want backs who can take advantage of these situations.

However, we have not consistently had the type of running back who could break the long one. This is because our running backs' 40-yard dash speed has varied from 4.6 seconds all the way up to 4.9 seconds. If we always had backs who could consistently beat the defenders one-on-one for the long gain, our offense would be even more explosive than it has been.

In addition to body balance and speed, other qualities we look for in our running backs are mental toughness, strong legs, and athletic hands. Many of our backs have not come to us with good hands, and this is a quality we have had to develop.

FULLBACK

We used to look for a fullback who was first a good blocker. We don't anymore. We still want fullbacks who can block, but first we look for people who can run with the ball. We don't want the opponents to be able to key on our running back.

NOT ALWAYS BETTER TALENT

You can see that while we always try to recruit the ideal talent, we aren't always able to get that talent. Because of our limited scholarship situation, I can honestly say that the majority of the time we have lined up offensively the opposition's defense has had better personnel. This is why we believe in our option package offense. You don't always have to have better talent to be successful. But you must have players who understand your system, players who are "winners," and players who can execute.

Now I would like to elaborate on three more points.

EXECUTION AND HABIT FORMATION

The first point concerns execution. When I was playing football and when I started to coach, I always heard that after a certain period of time you create a philosophy. But the more games I watched, the more I heard people say "Boy, they executed" if a team won or "Boy, they didn't execute" if a team lost. I believe you have to have an offensive philosophy, but you must also have execution. If ten players do their jobs on a play and one doesn't, that play could end up as a loss.

What creates good execution? We think that execution is created by constant repetition, establishing sound habit formation that creates a given conditioned reflex to a given situation.

To us, sound habit formation means solid habit formation. If we find that a player is doing something wrong, we will go back to check our practice schedules to see if enough time has been spent on the particular area of his weakness.

If we have spent enough time on what a player is having difficulty with, then maybe we haven't been teaching him properly. We always check ourselves, the coaching staff, first to see if we are in error before we go to the player. All of our practice schedules are saved, and this serves as a check-and-balance system for our coaching staff.

UTILIZE YOUR PLAYERS' TALENTS

A second main point is that you must take advantage of the things your players can do. This could refer to a group of players. For example, if we have a big offensive line, we will generally run more from the "I" formation. If we have a small offensive line, we will usually try to finesse the opposition more with the veer offense.

You must also take advantage of an individual player's abilities. For example, we had a great split end who could also throw the football. During his years at Carroll, the double pass became one of our biggest game-breaking plays.

REALIZE YOUR PLAYERS' LIMITATIONS

A third main point is that you should not try to do things offensively that your players are not capable of doing. Adhering to this principle won several games for us one season.

We had lost all of our quarterbacks to injuries by the fifth game of the season. There was no way we could run the option package offense in our final three games. Therefore, we reverted to the old single wing formation.

We were able to win our final three games using the single wing. Our defense gave up only 17 points in the three games and was superb. But we still would not have won without some production from our offense (41 points in the three games). This was not great offensive production, but it was much better than we would have gotten had we stuck with our regular option package offense.

No offense is as diverse and explosive as the option package. However, in this case, we had no choice but to use the single wing. We survived an unusual and difficult situation because we fit our offense to our personnel, not vice versa.

SUMMARY

You can see that what we would like in personnel and what we get are often quite different. But because we have won and consistently moved the ball, we are really sold on our option package offense. If your program is faced with limitations in size and material, the option package offense can win for you.

You have also seen that no matter how good his personnel, a coach must have players who can understand his system, players who are "winners," and players who can execute.

You have seen that the key to execution is sound habit formation. Finally, you have seen that a coach must use his players' individual and group talents and not force his players to do things they are incapable of doing.

CREATING A
SOLID OPTION
PACKAGE BASE

There are many things that go into the creation of a successful option package base. These things include the huddle, huddle break, numbering system, alignment and spacing, snap count, and formations. No play can be successful unless careful attention is given to these basics. Much of the success of a play is determined before the ball is ever snapped. Do not take your offensive base for granted. Organize it carefully and practice it.

HUDDLE

Our huddle is set up twelve to fifteen feet from the football. The quarterback is out in front because we sometimes use signals from the sideline to call the plays.

Only the quarterback talks in the huddle. He calls the formation, play, and count number *only once*. This is because we are using many audibles at the line of scrimmage and have only twenty-five seconds to get the play in.

This is the alignment of our huddle:

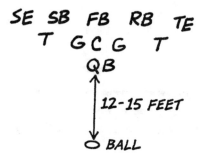

HUDDLE BREAK

Our receivers always leave the huddle first. After the receivers leave, the quarterback says "Break." All players then clap their hands, sprint to the ball, and assume a three-point stance.

You can tell a nondisciplined football team by the way its players break from the huddle. We very much believe in the discipline of sprinting to the ball. We want our players to sprint to the ball and let the other team know they are all "gunned up" and ready to go.

NUMBERING SYSTEM

The basic requirements of any numbering system are effectiveness and simplicity. In our system, holes to the right of center are even and holes to the left of center are odd.

$$_7O_5O_3O_1\square_2O_4O_6\;_8$$

When we flip-flop our line, our numbering system stays the same. We think it is less complicated this way and we firmly believe in the KISS (Keep It Simple, Stupid) philosophy. Anything we can do to simplify things for ourselves and our players, we will do.

Our fullback is always given the number "three." Our quarterback is always "one" and our running back is always "two."

We put numbers on our receivers so we can audible to them. Our split end is always 80, our slot back is always 40, and our tight end is always 90.

Any time a play is called, both a name and a number are given. For example, we might call the play "option 4." The name describes the action of the play and the number describes the area where the play is to be run.

The reason we give both a name and a number to every play is again simplicity. Most people who come to us know what an option is, what a sprint out is, what a trap is, etc. Once again, the name describes the action of the play and the number its location.

SPACING OR SPLITS

Our basic line splits are three feet between center and guards and three feet between guards and tackles. The tight end may be split either two, two and one-half, or three feet from the strong tackle, depending on the play. To get the required three-foot splits, our linemen spread out their arms when they arrive at the line of scrimmage.

$$3$$
$$2\tfrac{1}{2} \quad 3 \quad 3 \quad 3 \quad 3$$

O²O O □ O O
TE T   G   C G   T

Our splits may change against different types of defenses. For example, against a split defense, the splits would be three feet between the center and guards and two feet between the guards and tackles.

Against a 5-2 defense, we might split our tackles at three and one-half feet to widen out the defensive tackle. We will do this if we feel our center and guards can beat the opponent's nose guard and two linebackers.

Against an even defense we might move our guards' splits to three and one-half feet to put more pressure on the middle linebacker.

On the goal line, we move our line splits from three feet to one and one-half feet to keep the defense from penetrating the gaps and causing a broken play.

Thus, our line splits vary according to the defense and to what we are trying to do at a particular time. Our line splits are decided upon when we prepare our game plan.

BACKFIELD SPACING

In the "I" formation, our fullback is always lined up three and one-half yards from the ball. Our "I" back or running back is lined up directly behind the fullback.

In split backs, the fullback and running back are both lined up three and one-half yards from the ball. They line up behind our guards.

Our backs must be able to hit the hole quickly and maintain a four yards by one yard relationship (four yards deep and one yard outside the quarterback) on the pitch.

RECEIVER SPLITS

Our standard split for the split end is twelve to fifteen yards from the quick tackle. We never want our split end closer than six yards from the sideline. This is because many teams will use the sideline as an extra defensive man.

If the ball is spotted in the center of the field, the slot back should split the difference between the split end and quick tackle. However, more often the ball is spotted on a hash mark rather than in the center of the field. When the ball is spotted on a hash mark, we want our slot back aligned on the next hash mark.

SNAP COUNT

We always start our snap count with a color. We will have a true color, for example "red." Anything that follows "red" will be the play.

We say the color, then give a number, then say "down," "set," and "go." We can and will snap the ball on any of these except the number.

Our quarterbacks are always told to make sure every player is set for one second before getting under center for the snap. This complies with the rules. Then if we go on a color, we won't have problems with penalties.

Most of the time we will snap the ball on either a color, "down," or "set." If the ball is snapped on "go" it is because we either want to get motion or feel we can draw someone offside. We might also wait until "go" if we think we have been well scouted and if our opponents are ready for us to snap the ball quickly and are really digging in early.

We practice getting off the ball on color, "down," "set," and "go" for ten minutes every day.

Everything we do offensively in practice starts with a count and ends with a whistle, because that is what happens in a game.

MAIN FORMATIONS

Wide Slot

This is the number one formation of our option package from either the "I" or from split backs. We use this formation 70 to 80 percent of the time. The wide slot serves to reduce the defensive front and to set up a two-on-two situation with our wide receivers.

In the wide slot formation, the strongside line is always away from the slot. The quickside line is always to the slot.

"I" formation, slot right:

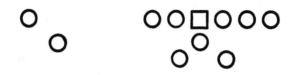

Split backs, slot left formation:

 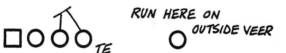

Wing Formation (Pro Set)

We also use a wing formation with both the "I" and split backs. Many people call this formation a pro set. We use the wing formation about 15 to 20 percent of the time. We use the formation for three reasons. First, we want to run off the tight end's block.

Second, we want to get our tight end into a one-on-one situation.

Third, we want to drag the tight end.

In the wing formation, our slot back is split wide, six yards from the sideline. The strongside line is always to the wing. The quickside line is always away.

"I" formation, wing left:

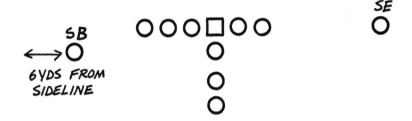

Split backs, wing right:

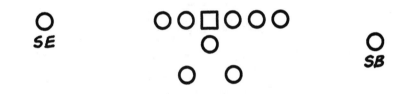

SUPPLEMENTARY FORMATIONS

Stack "I"

We will use the stack "I" formation with our tight end or slot back behind the quarterback. This is an effective formation for double-teaming on a quick and active nose guard.

Wishbone Formation

Our tight end is behind the quarterback in this formation. The wishbone formation enables us to force the defense into one-on-one coverage. It also allows the option pitch and creates the opportunity to run our tight end in motion on our pass-first, run-second option.

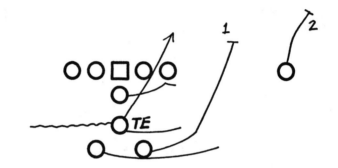

Trips Formation

The trips formation allows us to pressure the defense with three receivers to one side. Trips makes it easier to get the ball to our split end. If the defense plays a man across the board, crossing patterns are effective.

Quickside trips with crossing patterns:

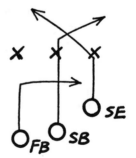

Fullback Formation

We use the fullback formation to one, set up strongside trips, and two, isolate our split end.

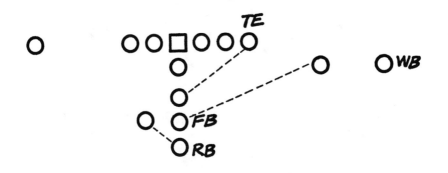

Short Slot Formation

This formation takes advantage of the talents of the tight end. First, the tight end can be used as a blocker in the offensive tackle hole. Second, the tight end can be run in motion. Third, since the tight end is off the line of scrimmage, he can release faster on pass routes without being held up.

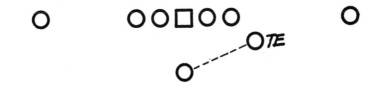

If the defense is balanced, you are in position to overpower it.

If the defense is unbalanced, run away.

You can run inside option or inside veer and get a soft read by the defensive end.

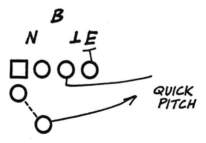

If the defensive end moves inside, run the quick pitch.

On the outside veer, you could have a mismatch if you have a big tight end.

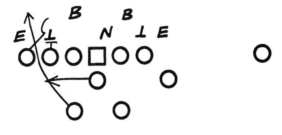

MULTIPLE FORMATIONS

In all, we use seven formations—the wide slot, the wing or pro set, the stack "I," the wishbone, trips, the short slot, and the fullback formation.

We use multiple formations because multiple formations cause defenses to make multiple adjustments. We don't like to play teams that use a great many formations. When you spend a lot of time preparing for multiple formations, it is hard to spend enough time on tackling technique.

Also, if you don't have superior manpower it is unwise to simply set up and show the defense where you are going. It is best to keep the defense off balance. This will mean more work on execution, but it will also mean more adjustments for the defenses you will encounter.

EMPHASIZE ONE

We always put more emphasis on one formation for a particular game. We do this to nullify something the opposition does well defensively.

For example, in 1981, we were facing a team that had a very quick and active nose guard. He had given us a great deal of trouble the previous year. We had a big, slow freshman center and there was no way we felt he could handle their nose guard.

Therefore, we emphasized the stack "I" formation in our game plan. We aligned our slot back behind our quarterback to double on the nose guard. Our slot back had been a fullback in junior college and was an excellent blocker. The move paid off as we moved the ball well and ended up winning 38-3.

4

ESTABLISHING
A SOUND
BLOCKING SYSTEM

PHILOSOPHY

Our philosophy of offensive line-blocking centers around a belief in guard-tackle calls at the line of scrimmage. These guard-tackle calls will allow the best blocking angles against various defensive sets.

Our philosophy is also developed on the theory that defenses will 90 percent of the time be in one of three looks—an odd, an even, or a split.

We also believe that a defensive man only can play an offensive lineman one of three ways—head up, inside, or outside.

In our system, the guards will make the calls for the one, two, three, and four holes. The tackles will make the calls for the five, six, seven, and eight holes. For this system to succeed, false calls must be made at the line of scrimmage away from the point of attack.

TRAP-BLOCKING RULES

Our trap-blocking is assignment blocking with two rules. First, on the short trap, always trap the defensive tackle. Second, on the long trap, always trap the outside man on the line of scrimmage.

STACK RULE

Our stack rule is based on the philosophy that the defense can only stack in six areas.

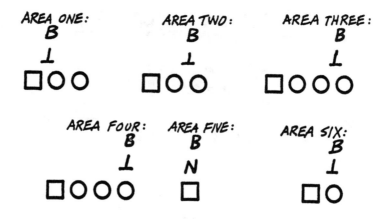

Our rule says that the two offensive linemen closest to the stack will double-team the down lineman and read the linebacker. If the linebacker comes in an offensive lineman's area, the lineman will slide off and block the backer.

We call this block a Combo Block, and we feel we must move the down lineman two yards off the ball.

If we get a stack in the fourth area, we will block the inside area with our tight end and the quarterback will read the outside area in our option game.

If we are having trouble blocking this fourth area, we will go to our loaded block on their outside man.

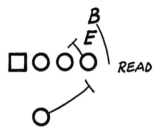

Thus, our blocking system and philosophy are based on the understanding of our true-and-false call system, our stack rule, and our trap assignment system. This system allows our normally smaller offensive linemen a good opportunity to block the opponent's bigger defensive linemen.

EXECUTION

Before we get into the execution of our Man Block, let me emphasize that we must execute on the *sprint* off the ball. Our blockers must have their necks in and eyes looking ahead, not down. Vision is very important to execution.

We use what is called the Crowther Blocking Technique in the teaching of our Man Block. We feel this type of blocking best enables our offensive linemen to utilize both upper body and leg strength.

Because of recent rule changes that permit more use of the hands in blocking, we ask our linemen to "bench press" up with both hands to the sternum area. Thus, the hands take the initial blow more than the chin.

STANCE

The stance is like the foundation of a house. If the foundation is not solid, the house collapses. Likewise, a player cannot get off the ball or maintain a good block without a proper stance.

This is why we have a stance drill where each player's stance is evaluated by a coach. This is also why we have a check-off list for the stance. We give the player a check-off list for the stance and then strive to have him get comfortable within that framework.

In the Man Block, our linemen should have their feet the width of their shoulders. Second, their feet should have a toe-instep relationship. (Centers are more square, i.e. toe to toe.) If the player is tall, there should be more of a toe-heel relationship.

The player's power leg should be at a right angle with his heels slightly above the grass. The player's back and shoulders should be square with his buttocks slightly higher than his shoulders.

The player's neck should be bulled, enabling him to see the defensive man's position. His off hand should rest on the knee. His down hand should be extended slightly in front of his shoulder in a finger bridge, not a knuckle bridge. This is because we want our linemen to move right or left and pull. If we just wanted to fire out straight ahead, our players would use a knuckle bridge with all their weight forward.

Our check-off list for the stance includes:

1. The neck must be in and the head up.
2. When the down hand goes down, the shoulders must be parallel.
3. When the down hand is down in the finger bridge, both knees should be straight—not turned in or turned out. The shoulders should also be straight—not turned in or out.
4. The player should be able to remove his down hand and still have balance.

THREE-STEP PROCEDURE

Once the player has developed a sound stance, he is ready to begin the three-step procedure of the Man Block. On his first step, the blocker drives off his power leg and takes a short (six-inch) step. On his first step, the blocker should roll over his front knee. This enables him to stay low.

The blocker's second step should also be a six-inch step. It is very important that his second step goes beyond the first step, so a toe-heel relationship can be maintained. Realistically, contact is going to be made on this second step.

The third step is a driving step. When the blocker comes out of the third step, his feet should be in a toe-to-toe relationship.

The blocker's back should remain flat. His neck should be "bulled," his head up and his eyes on the defensive man's breast. The blocker's striking point is in the defender's breast. The blocker should strike this area with his hands and chin. If this technique is executed properly, the blocker's hands should always make first contact.

The blocker must learn to explode into the defender and at the same time "bench press" up with the hands. The neck must remain "bulled" while the chin is making contact with the defender's breast.

A main coaching point here is that the blocker must never make contact with the top of the defender's helmet. The blocker is much more susceptible to injury in this position.

HOW WE TEACH HITTING

After our players learn the three-step procedure, we work on hitting. We teach that there are three areas with which the blocker can strike. The first is with his chin in the direction of the ball. If the play is straight ahead, the chin should hit the defender's sternum. The second hitting area is with the hands. If the blocker "bench presses" up with both hands properly, his hands will hit the defender before his chin does. The third hitting area is with the shoulder pads. This is where a player's hitting power is.

We begin teaching the hitting phase of the Man Block by having the players kneel. They are told to put their chins into a dummy or a person and "bench press" up with the hands. When they do this, they get the feeling of the proper position of the head, hands, and shoulder pads.

The players also learn something else by blocking on their knees. They learn that all of their weight is forward, and this makes it impossible to deliver a truly effective blow.

If our blockers are going to stay on their feet, they must learn to *bring their hips with them* and rotate the hips up through the defensive man.

DRIVE PHASE

The drive phase is the final phase of the Man Block. Here the blocker must drive the defender off the line of scrimmage. At the same time, he must work to position himself between the ball carrier and the defender while keeping his neck "bulled" to aid in positioning.

After the hands "bench press" up through the defensive player, the legs and feet should begin driving in short, quick steps. This will enable the blocker to move the defender off the line of scrimmage or at least create a stalemate. The blocker must keep his legs driving. This allows him to maintain contact when the defensive man tries to move to the ball carrier. Emphasis should be placed on blocking for four seconds, the average time of one play.

BLOCKING DRILLS

Board Drill

We stress several blocking fundamentals in the board drill. First, the blocker must keep his legs under his body. Second, his legs must remain the width of his shoulders. Third, the blocker must drive with his legs after upper extremity contact.

The board we use is six feet long and twenty-two inches wide. We use a board this width because it teaches the blocker to keep his feet approximately the width of his shoulders. If he doesn't, he will lose his balance.

A dummy is set at the front of the board. The blocker is also at the front of the board facing the dummy. Behind the board are the center, quarterback, and running back. On the signal by the quarterback, the blocker drives off and blocks the dummy completely up through the six feet of the board. Meanwhile, the quarterback takes the snap and hands off to the running back. The running back then cuts off the block.

To execute a successful block, the offensive lineman must bring his hips and legs with him on initial contact.

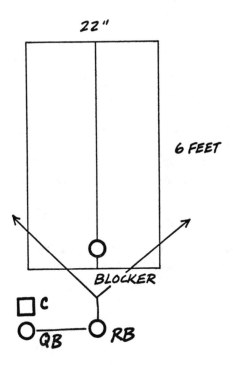

Two-Man Sled Drill

We have two drills with the two-man sled. The first drill teaches the actual explosion or hit in an upward manner. Our players learn this by blocking the two-man sled up a hill. Again, we are stressing upward explosion through the defensive man.

The second drill stresses another important fundamental—an offensive lineman must bring his hips with him to maintain balance. Our linemen learn this by blocking the two-man sled down a hill.

In both drills, we always start with a count and end with a whistle because that is what happens on every offensive play.

Blocking the Gap

We also call this the Seam Block. We feel the Seam Block is the most difficult block to teach. Every offensive lineman must be able to execute the Seam Block many, many times in a given game.

Begin teaching the Seam Block by placing a dummy or blocking shield to the inside gap of the offensive lineman. Explain that the blocker must stop penetration to the inside gap.

Next, take the blocker's chin and place it on the outside of the seam area. Show the blocker how it is very easy for him to be beaten in this position.

Then have the blocker stick his chin into the defender's inside breast. Stress that the blocker must have his neck in and head up. As the blocker gets his chin into the defender's inside breast, he must "bench press" up with his hands into the defender's rib cage.

The head up will stop penetration. The "bench press" up into the rib cage will stop the defender's momentum.

Finally, teach the blocker to turn his buttocks upfield and Man Block the defender.

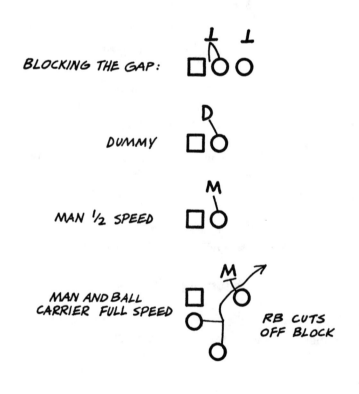

Also, walk through the importance of the near foot in the Seam Block. If the blocker steps with the far foot, the defender will have the seam. If the blocker steps with the near foot, he will stop penetration of the seam.

We believe there is no easy way to teach the Seam Block. It must be learned by constant repetition.

After walking through the block, add a dummy. Then, add a defender and have the blocker go half-speed. Finally, add a ball carrier who cuts to the outside of the Seam Block. This drill is done at full speed.

We have found that it is easier to block right to left on the Seam Block than left to right. This is because most players are right-handed and can "bench press" up easier with their right hand.

Combo Block

We use the Combo Block in three situations—against split defenses between guard and tackle, to block the five and six holes against odd or even defenses, and to block against stack defenses.

Our technique involves having both offensive linemen step with his near foot. Both linemen then stick their chins into the defender's breast area on their sides. Each blocker must keep his neck in and head up in order to be able to read the linebacker. As they make contact, both blockers must "bench press" up with the hands. Finally, both blockers must work to get their legs square to their shoulders and to keep their balance.

Both blockers should make contact with the defensive man at the same time. Each must turn his inside hip inside, and they must get butt-to-butt so the defender will not be able to break the seam.

The initial goal of each lineman is to drive the defender two yards off the ball and block the linebacker if he is in that lineman's area.

Our Combo Block stack drill is set up so the blocker has to go inside out. Then a ball carrier is added, and he cuts off the block on the linebacker. This drill is usually done live.

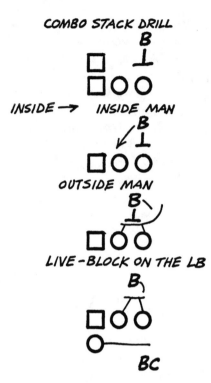

Switch Block

We use the Switch Block against one-linebacker defenses. The block is between the center and guard away from playside. We start to playside and then switch to backside to get an angle.

We will also use the Switch Block to break down the false key of the middle linebacker keying the center. If the linebacker steps up, we give a false key when running outside.

The center should go first. His first step is with his near foot. He sticks his chin into the defender's near breast. The center then "bench presses" up with both hands and drives the defender out to create a gap.

Our biggest problem has been that the center sometimes has not driven the defender far enough to create a gap. We are not happy with a stalemate.

The guard steps with his near foot *upfield*—not around. He then gets his chin into the defender's near breast, "bench presses" up, and drives him out. The guard must also create a gap.

Our biggest problem with the guard as to technique has been that he sometimes gets overextended. If he steps too far he will go to his knees when he makes the hit. The first and second steps are *short* steps.

Over Block

We use the Over Block 90 percent of the time against an odd defense with an over-backer stunt.

This is a two-on-two block between the guard and center. They are responsible for the nose guard and the backside linebacker.

The center has two advantages. First, he knows the snap count. Second, he knows the direction of the play. The center must get off the ball and take his lead step six inches in the direction of the ball. There must be no false step.

The center snaps the ball, steps with his near foot, and reads the hip to playside of the nose guard. If the hip is coming to playside, he must get his chin to the inside breast of the nose guard. The center then turns his buttocks upfield. He must stop penetration by the nose guard.

If the hip is away from playside, the center must "bench press" up at the outside breast to stop the nose guard's momentum. The center then slides off, gets upfield, and blocks the linebacker.

The guard keys the far hip of the nose guard. He steps with his near foot, sticks his chin into the defender's sternum, "bench presses" up with both hands, and turns his buttocks upfield.

Sometimes the center gets too anxious and doesn't hit the nose guard. He must "bench press" up at the nose guard before going to the linebacker.

Also, when the far hip is to the guard, the center must get his chin across to the far breast, then "bench press" up and get his buttocks upfield.

Slide Block

This block is the same as the Over Block, but it is between the guard and tackle rather than the guard and center. The techniques of the Over Block and the Slide Block are the same.

We use the Slide Block against the slant-scrape stunt.

The offensive tackle steps with his outside foot and keys the near hip of the defensive tackle. If the near hip (or outside hip) comes to the defensive tackle, the offensive tackle must Man Block him. If the outside hip is away on the slant tackle, he must "bench press" up on the tackle with his hands to stop momentum. This allows the guard to get his chin across to the inside breast.

The offensive guard steps to the down tackle. He keys the far hip. If the hip is in, he puts his chin into the defender's sternum, "bench presses" up, and gets his body upfield. If the defender's hip is away, the guard gets upfield to block the linebacker.

Green Block

We like to use this block against a 5-2 defense. The Green Block does two things. First, it gives us an angle when we are running to the two and four holes. Second, it gives the linebacker a false key.

The Green Block is a cross block between the guard and tackle. The guard goes first. He steps with his near foot. He then blocks the inside rib cage with his chin and "bench presses" up. The guard must create a gap. We do not want a stalemate.

The tackle steps with his near foot. He blocks the sternum area of the man inside with his chin and "bench presses" up with his hands. He must knock the inside man down.

Red Block

The Red Block is between the guard and tackle. It is a come-around block. The only time we use the Red Block is against a split defense.

The offensive tackle should Seam Block the defensive tackle.

The offensive guard uses pulling technique and blocks the linebacker. When the guard pulls, his target is the outside breast with his chin. When he gets into the defensive man, the guard must turn his buttocks upfield and square up. He must move his feet to stay with the defender. This is not an easy block. Because the linebacker is inside out, the guard must clear himself with his left arm.

Position Block

The only time we use the Position Block is when we Red Block against a split defense. The Position Block is a center block. We do this when we are trying to create a gap to get the ball to the fullback on the option.

The center steps and checks the two hole. If the linebacker is in the two hole, the center must block him.

If the linebacker is outside, the center blocks the backside linebacker.

TWO TRAP RULES FOR GUARDS

If we are in a short trap with the fullback, the guard always traps the defensive tackle. If we are in a long trap with anyone besides the fullback, the guard always traps the outside man on the line of scrimmage.

PULLING GUARD TECHNIQUE ON TRAPS

The guard gets into his normal stance. The guard should not lean in the direction he is going to pull. This is easy to key.

The guard then rips his arm in the direction he is going to pull. This is an overexaggerated rip. This rip will pull the rest of his body around. After he pulls, the guard must stay low and *sprint* to the defensive man because the quicker the trap, the greater the gain.

The guard should step down the line of scrimmage, not off the line of scrimmage. If we are going to trap inside-out, the guard's chin must be inside the defensive man.

When you trap, you must either knock the defensive man down or create a gap.

TRUE CALL SYSTEM

The true call is the call made at the point of attack. The guard always calls the one, two, three, and four holes. The tackle always calls the five, six, seven, and eight holes.

Going into a game, our line always has two options on how we are going to block on a particular play. This is called our check-off list.

For example, on our option three and four against a 50 defense, we might have the choice of: (1) Veer Block, or (2) Slide Block. Option three and four against a 40 defense might be: (1) Veer Block, or (2) T Block. Option three and four against a split defense could be: (1) Combo Block, or (2) Red Block. Our check-off list is compiled in our game plan from week to week.

In addition to knowing the weekly check-off list, our linemen must pass a weekly test. They must be able to recognize and diagram every defensive set they might see.

For example, on a 50 defense they must know a straight 50 Okie, a 50 Eagle, a 50 Eagle stack, a 50 offset gap, and a 50 offset stack.

Our linemen must also be able to recognize and diagram all the different sets from the 40 defense and the split defense.

FALSE CALLS

False calls are made away from the point of attack. If every lineman does not make a call, it is easy for the defense to pick up where the ball is going. Our false calls and true calls are similar. We never call out a name, always a letter. For example, a Veer Block might be "V," a Red Block "R," and a Green Block "G."

If you were listening to our linemen make their true and false calls, it might sound like they were rehearsing the alphabet. We change the letters on our calls every year.

PASS-BLOCKING SYSTEM

We spend ten to fifteen minutes a day on pass blocking. On our sprint-out and play-action passes, we use the same blocking calls at the point of attack that we use for the rest of our offense.

We must also block the backside to protect the quarterback. Quarterbacks are more likely to be injured when they are hit from the backside. We preach this constantly.

We have a guard and a tackle on the backside to Cup Block. On the Cup Block, the lineman steps with his inside foot and turns to protect the inside seam. He must force the defensive man to the outside, front the defensive man, and stay with him. He must keep his feet moving.

The Cup Block:

$$\varphi \, \varphi \, \square$$

Many times when we are reading linebackers in different defenses, blocking the backside will be the open lineman. Against a 50 defense, the open lineman is the guard.

Against a 40 defense, the open lineman is the center.

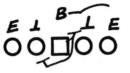

Against a split defense, the center keys the backside line-backer. If he comes, the center must block him. If he goes to the pass, the center blocks the backside.

This is the frontside blocking against a 50 defense:

The guard and tackle double and read the backer. If the backer comes inside, the guard blocks him.

If the backer goes outside, the tackle blocks him.

40 defense—man block.

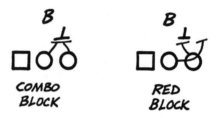

Split defense blocking schemes:

COMBO
BLOCK

RED
BLOCK

On a 40 defense, middle linebacker stunt, the center and guard double on the defensive tackle and read the middle linebacker. If the linebacker comes inside, the center blocks him. If the linebacker is outside, the guard blocks him.

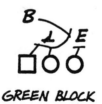

GREEN BLOCK

PASS-BLOCKING SYNOPSIS

1. It is very important on playside that our uncovered linemen do not show pass.
2. Much of the time the guard and tackle Cup Block to

force the defensive man to the outside. They must keep their feet moving. When they are flat-footed, they will be beaten.

3. It is also very important that the backside uncovered linemen (90 percent of the time the guard and center) protect the backside so the quarterback doesn't get hit from the backside.

4. If we are in a wide slot, the person with the toughest job is the quick tackle. He usually has a man on his head and he can't let that man beat him inside or outside. He must fire out and block that defensive man.

COACHING

THE "I" FORMATION

RUNNING GAME

PHILOSOPHY

The philosophy of the "I" formation running game is to maintain possession of the football. If your offensive line can block the line of scrimmage, you can be successful with the "I."

The "I" formation has certain advantages. First, it allows you to take advantage of that one outstanding running back. Sometimes it is easier to find that one outstanding running back and then get a hard-nosed fullback and teach him to block. The "I" is also easier to execute than the veer because most plays are between the quarterback and the running back.

BLAST

The blast must be blocked four ways for the play to succeed.

"Y" BLOCK

One way to block the blast is with the "Y" Block. This is a double-team block at the point of attack. The center and guard double on the nose guard. The fullback lead blocks on the linebacker.

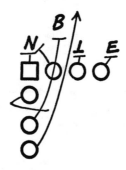

GREEN BLOCK

A second block used in the blast is the Green Block, a cross block between the guard and tackle. The offensive guard blocks out on the defensive tackle. The offensive tackle blocks down on the linebacker. The fullback runs to the outside hip of the center and double-team blocks on the nose guard. The quarterback reverse pivots and continues to the corner with a good fake. The "I" back must be taught to fall over his front knee and not take a false step. The "I" back cuts off the block of the tackle and runs to daylight.

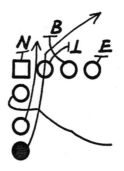

MAN BLOCK

A third way to block the blast is with the "M" or Man Block. The fullback still doubles on the nose guard. Against a "5" defense, the nose guard must be doubled at all times.

The "I" back should be running north and south so his body is square. If the "I" back goes into the hole square, he can quickly cut right or left to daylight.

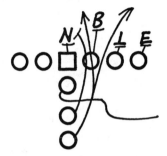

VEER BLOCK

A fourth block used in the blast is the Veer Block. This block is used to get an inside-out angle. The center and guard double-team block the nose guard. The offensive tackle blocks down on the linebacker. The fullback trap blocks out on the defensive tackle.

This is a fairly simple play if the quarterback reverse pivots. There should not be minus yardage or a fumble on the play. The quarterback takes the snap and drop steps to get depth. He then brings the ball in and reverses out.

The "I" back should run with his inside arm up. After the quarterback places the ball in the "I" back's stomach, the "I" back should roll his stomach over the ball. Most fumbles are caused by the back failing to roll his stomach over the ball.

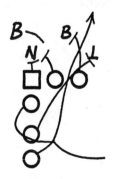

GAME PLAN

How many ways the blast will be blocked is determined in game plan. The blocks—"Y", Green, Man and Veer—are called at the line of scrimmage.

ATTACKING THE 5-2 DEFENSE

Ninety percent of the time, you will be facing one of three defenses—a 5-2 (odd), a 4-3 (even), or a split. Against a 5-2, you must know who are your opponent's weakest linebacker and defensive tackle. The target area to run to is the outside hip of the guard.

ATTACKING THE 4-3 DEFENSE

Against a 4-3 defense, the center and guard should double on the defensive tackle. They should try to get movement upfield two yards, and then one should pick up the linebacker.

On the "Y" Block against the 4-3, the offensive tackle and fullback should double-team the defensive end. This is a difficult seam block. The offensive tackle steps with his outside foot and blocks the outside breast of the defensive end. The defensive end has been told, "Don't get hooked inside." When the defensive end steps out, it allows the fullback to block him.

When the "I" back gets the ball, he must read the linebacker. The target area is the gap between the offensive guard and offensive tackle.

The "Y" Block against the 4-3:

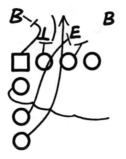

VEER BLOCK AGAINST A 4-3

The Veer Block against a 4-3 is like our Combo Block. When we are trapping inside, it is called a Veer Block. There are two double-team blocks and a trap.

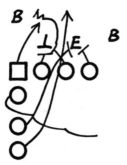

MAN BLOCK AGAINST A 4-3

Use the Man Block against a 4-3 defense if you have a bigger and more physical team. The fullback must lead through the hole and block the middle linebacker.

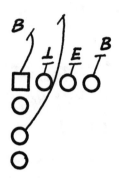

ATTACKING THE SPLIT DEFENSE

To attack the split defense, you must reduce the defensive front from eight players to seven. You should not run against an eight-man front. Teams who do not reduce the front should be superior physically.

The defensive front can be reduced in two ways. First, you can use a wide formation and get a two-on-one situation against the corner back.

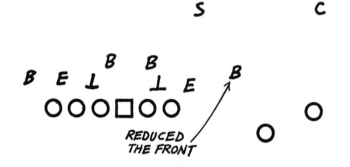

The second way to reduce the front is to split the tight end out wide:

TE

As soon as the front is reduced to seven, run to the reduced front. We run blast and prefer to Combo Block it. Double on the defensive tackle and read the linebacker. If the linebacker comes in, the guard must take him. If the defensive tackle goes outside, the offensive tackle must block him. You are striving for an inside-out blocking angle.

The guard always steps with his near foot. He must get his face mask into the defender's near breast and his pads into the stomach area. The tackle steps with his near foot and gets his face mask into the defender's breast area on his side. The defensive down tackle must be driven two yards off the line of scrimmage so a good rotation of the hips is needed.

The "I" back winds back off the center's block. The seal will provide an alley to run outside. This is an effective play because defensive people must have inside-out pursuit to the ball. This play cuts off inside pursuit.

The Combo Block versus a split defense:

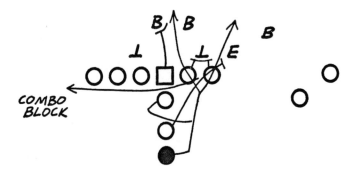

LINEBACKER OUT FAST

If the linebacker comes out fast, use the windback.

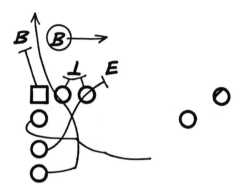

If the linebacker stunts, the play should be Man-Blocked.

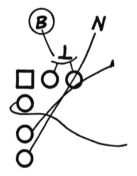

RED BLOCK

Many teams will Red Block against a split defense. The offensive tackle blocks down on the defensive tackle. The guard pulls outside.

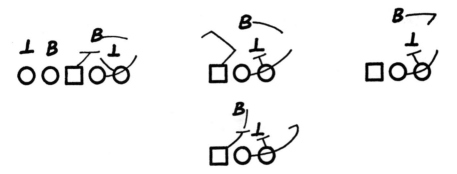

The center position blocks and reads the strongside linebacker. If the strongside linebacker moves outside, the center blocks the backside linebacker. Then, there will be only one running lane.

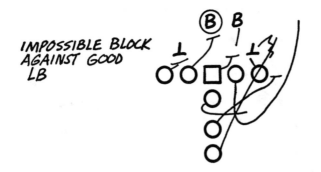

SHORT-YARDAGE AND GOAL SITUATIONS

The blast is an effective short-yardage and goal-line play. Most defensive teams will be in either a 6-5 stack or a 6-5 wide in goal line situations.

Diagram of 6-5 stack:

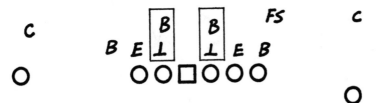

Diagram of a 6-5 wide:

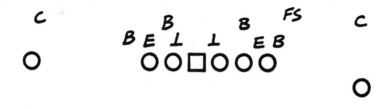

You must know how tough the defensive team's linebacker and offside tackle are. If your fullback can handle the linebacker, Man Block the play. If your fullback is going to have trouble with the linebacker, use the Veer Block.

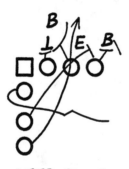

VEER BLOCK

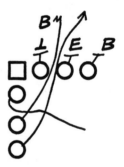

END DOUBLE WITH FB

ATTACKING THE 40 DEFENSE

If the defense plays a 40 defense on the goal line or in short-yardage situations, block the blast the same way you do against a 4-3 defense. You can "Y" Block it, Veer Block it, or once in a while Man Block it.

OFFSET

If the defense is using an offset, run away from the offset.

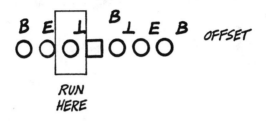

SUMMARY

The blast is a great number one play from the "I" formation. The defense *can* put six people in the middle and stop the blast. If the defense does this, simply run somewhere else.

OPTION (3 OR 4 IN OUR SYSTEM)

We will Veer Block and run the blast. Everything inside is the same on the option. The defensive man cannot tell immediately if the play is option or blast unless he looks at the quarterback's pivot. If the quarterback reverse pivots, the play is blast. If the quarterback steps out at a 45-degree angle, the play is option.

COACHING THE OPTION FROM THE "I" FORMATION

The quarterback should take a 45-degree step. He *must* have his eyes on the first read area. The natural tendency is to take a step, with the head following the step. The quarterback cannot do this. He must keep his eyes on the target area.

When the quarterback takes his second step, his feet should be in a toe-instep relationship. The quarterback then takes a two-step ride to determine whether or not he will give the fullback the ball.

Once the quarterback's steps have been taught, put in a fullback and have the fullback run to the target area. The fullback comes out of his stance, rolls over the near knee, gets off quickly, and stays low. He then runs to the target area.

There are many opinions as to what the target area is. Our fullbacks are taught to run to the outside leg of the offensive guard.

To emphasize the target area, employ a light pylon in order to prevent injuries.

Have the fullback and quarterback work on the mesh. The other quarterbacks should be the defensive tackles so they can learn in what ways the defensive tackle can play. The defensive tackle can come down, come upfield, or stay.

FIRST READ

If the defensive tackle comes down, the quarterback should pull the ball out. If the tackle comes upfield, the quarterback must give the ball to the fullback. If the tackle stays on the line of scrimmage, the quarterback gives the ball to the fullback.

SECOND READ

If the defensive end comes down hard, the quarterback should pitch the ball. If the end goes upfield, the quarterback must turn upfield fast and get yardage. If the defensive end stays at the line of scrimmage, the quarterback should run to the end's inside shoulder. This will force the defensive end to decide quickly whether to take the quarterback or the pitch man.

The pitch man should be 4×1. This means that there should be four yards between the quarterback and the pitch man. This way, one defensive man cannot cover both of them. The pitch man should be one yard outside so the quarterback can see him and get him the ball.

THE PITCH

The quarterback should not turn his head when he pitches the ball. If he does, he has no way to see the defensive man coming and protect himself.

Give your quarterbacks peripheral vision tests. The pitch man should be only one yard outside (4×1). If the quarterback cannot see the pitch man in his peripheral vision, he should not pitch the ball.

An option quarterback must be a quick thinker. He must have quick, conditioned reflexes. This can be taught.

FUMBLES

There are going to be times when the ball will be fumbled on the pitch. However, you cannot allow a mistake to take you away from what you are trying to do.

AN ALLEY

When there is an alley, the quarterback must get upfield. He must also determine the *danger zone*. If the quarterback is upfield and being cornered by more than one tackler, he should slide down. Persuading the quarterback to do this is difficult because of his natural human pride and courage. However, it is a necessity.

In college football, the quarterback should try to get upfield as quickly as possible and not cut back against the grain. The quarterback can get away with cutting back across the grain in high school, but his chances of getting hurt in college games are much greater.

Some coaches do not run the option because they feel their quarterbacks will get hurt. However, a drop-back quarterback is much more susceptible to injury if he is sacked from the blind side than an option quarterback is running the football. We have never had a quarterback get hurt on the line of scrimmage running the option—but this has to be coached.

WIDE RECEIVER BLOCK

From the pro set, the receiver block is very important to the success of the option. The receiver must get off the ball *hard* and create a cushion. The defensive back should be reading the pass. The receiver must not break down until the defensive back starts to come up.

The receiver should bring his hips on the block so he does not get overextended. He should try to stay in the defensive back's face and keep his feet moving. It is up to the back to cut off the receiver's block. The taller the receiver, the better the block will be.

TIGHT END BLOCK

The tight end takes a three-step release and reads. If the cornerback retreats, the tight end should block the safety. If the cornerback rolls up, the tight end blocks the corner inside-out.

If the play is run to the "one" receiver side, most defenses will not roll the corner unless by adjustment in pre-snap read. If the defense does roll the corner, the play should be changed at the line of scrimmage to lead option. If the play is not changed, it is Man Blocked.

SIX KEYS

There are six keys to a successful option: (1) The quarterback; (2) The dive back; (3) The pitch man; (4) The receiver's block; (5) The seal inside by the line; and (6) The ability to throw off option action. The defense can make things very tough without the threat of a pass. The pass does not have to be long. A short pass can turn into a long gain.

ATTACKING THE 5-2 DEFENSE

Because of the slant scrape and over scrape, the Veer Block has become a difficult block against the 5-2 defense. It is difficult to get the offensive tackle down inside.

Diagram of the Veer Block:

The Slant Scrape:

The Over Scrape:

When the defense began bringing the tackle in hard and the linebacker out, a new blocking scheme called the Slide Block was formed.

In the Slide Block, the guard and tackle both key the far hip of the defensive tackle. The guard should get his face mask across and block the outside breast of the defensive tackle. The offensive tackle must get a piece of the defensive tackle. Both the guard and tackle read the linebacker. If the defensive tackle slants down inside, the offensive tackle blocks the linebacker.

If the defensive tackle stays, the play is blocked in this manner:

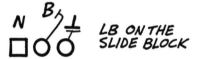

If the defensive tackle comes down inside, the quarterback should pull the ball and go to the second read. The fullback must bang in hard while the "I" back looks for the pitch. The instant this happens, there will be a one-on-one situation with the nose guard without the Over Block.

OVER BLOCK

If the play is Over-Blocked, it is blocked just like the Slide Block. The center steps with his near foot to playside. He keys the far hip of the nose guard.

The offensive guard steps into the gap. He keys the far hip of the nose guard, gets his facemask into the far breast, and works his buttocks upfield.

LINEBACKER READ

When you see a 5-2 defense, except a slant scrape or an over scrape. Our call is "Option four, linebacker read."

The first read is now the linebacker. The second read is the defensive end. The defensive tackle must be doubled and driven two yards off the line of scrimmage. The other side Over Blocks.

If the linebacker steps out, the fullback gets the ball. If the linebacker steps up, the fullback must block him, and the quarterback goes to the second option, the defensive end.

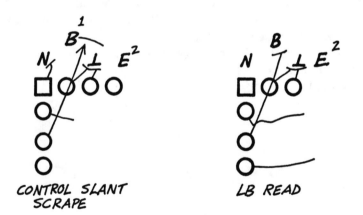

CONTROL SLANT
SCRAPE

LB READ

ATTACKING THE 50 STACK

Against a 50 stack, the ball should be run to the quick side. Double down on the defensive tackle and read the linebacker. You are now limited to one read at the line of scrimmage.

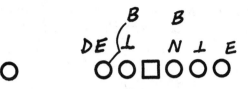

ATTACKING THE EAGLE

Against a double eagle, the problem is getting a Man Block on the nose guard.

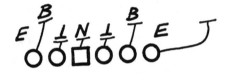

ATTACKING THE EAGLE STACK

Some teams will try an Eagle Stack to force the center to block the nose guard man-to-man. The defensive tackles are over the guards and the linebackers are outside. When the defense does this, run to the quick side. Combo Block the defensive tackle. There is now one read.

The Eagle Stack:

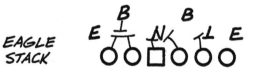

One read:

ATTACKING THE 4-3 PRO

In this alignment, the defensive ends are in and the linebackers are out. To attack the 4-3 pro, use the Veer Block or "T" Block.
  The Veer Block:

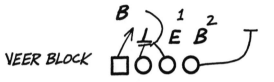

The "T" Block:

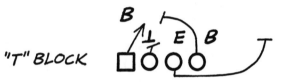

ATTACKING THE 4-3 COLLEGE

First, try to read it. Split the tackle a little further and try to get the ball to the fullback. We call this "option four, linebacker read." If the defensive tackle is tough and you are having trouble sealing him, use some misdirection.

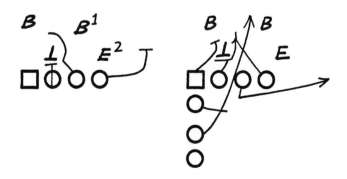

DEFENSIVE TACKLE OVER CENTER

If the defensive team uses a 4-3 with the defensive tackle over center, the center must block that man when you are running to the tight-end side. Because of this, we will change the play at the line of scrimmage and run to the quick side. This allows a double-team block on the tackle.

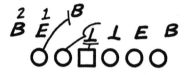

ATTACKING THE SPLIT DEFENSE

Again, never allow a team to play you in an eight-man front. Run wide slot and throw until the defense moves out of the eight-man front. If the defense stays in the eight-man front, it is giving you a two-on-one advantage with the cornerback. You can't ask for any better odds than that. Use lead option pass and throw, even if it's every down, until the defense adjusts.

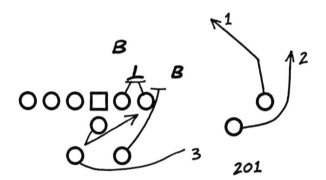

The minute the defense adjusts, run the option. Combo on the defensive tackle and read the end.

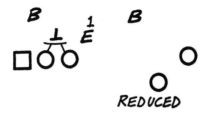

REDUCED

FLASH CARDS

You will often find multiple defenses that foul up your quarterback reads and force the quarterback to attack the strength of the defense.

To combat this, we square out the area we plan to run to against any possible defense. We make flash cards and show our quarterbacks the defenses. The cards tell us what the defense is and where we are going to attack the defense. These flash cards have been a great help to our program.

WINDBACK

The windback keeps the defense's linebackers at home. It also allows you to seal more effectively. You must run the windback to keep the option package offense going. You are trying to make the defense think you are running the option.

When the fullback gets the ball, he should run to the target area and then wind the play back.

The quarterback should get his hands in and run to the defensive end's shoulder. If he does this correctly, he will hold the defensive end and the linebacker. It is much easier to seal if the linebacker stays home.

The "I" back must be an actor. He should stay 4×1 and be looking at the quarterback for the ball.

WINDBACK AGAINST ONE
LINEBACKER DEFENSES

The windback is very effective against one linebacker defenses. The play can be run to both sides.

Windback against a one linebacker defense:

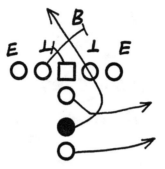

WINDBACK AGAINST A 5-2 DEFENSE

The fullback reads the offensive tackle's block on the linebacker.

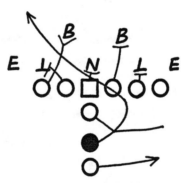

WINDBACK AGAINST A 4-3 DEFENSE

Defensive teams will usually key the linebacker on the fullback. If the defense is reading the fullback, run the windback.

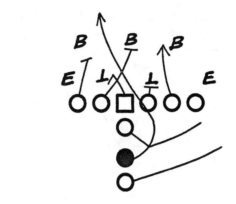

If the defense keys the center, the linebacker will be kept out of the play. Then run wide.

RUN WIDE

WINDBACK AGAINST A SPLIT DEFENSE

Fire out, Combo Block, and read the playside linebacker. You must create movement and you must create a seam. Double the tackle and get movement for two yards. The fullback should read the linebacker. If the backer moves out, the fullback should wind back off the center's block.

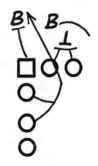

If the linebacker steps up, the fullback should not wind it back. The fullback should instead go right behind the double-team block of the guard and tackle.

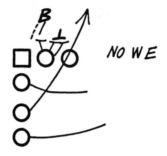

TRAP (31-32 IN OUR SYSTEM)

The trap does several things. It gives misdirection and deception. It gives quarterback influence to the defensive end and tackle. It helps keep the linebackers at home.

The trap can be a great play if a team is running the option effectively. The first time we put the play in, our fullback gained a school record of 278 yards rushing.

Again, our trap rules are: If the defense is in an odd front (5-2), we will trap the defensive tackle; if the defense is in a split or 4-3 defense, we will trap the widest man on the line of scrimmage 90 percent of the time. We will only change this by game plan.

Diagram of a 32 trap against a 5-2 defense:

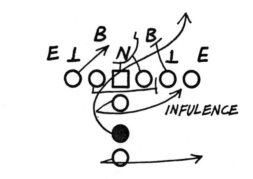

REDUCED FRONT

Sometimes we will see a reduced front against a "five" defense. If we see an Eagle Stack, we like to trap to the reduced front. We will trap the outside man. We fire out and Combo Block the tackle and linebacker. If we trap the "two" area, we call the play "32 trap."

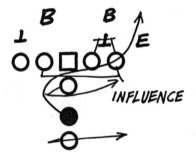

TRAP AGAINST A 4-3 DEFENSE

We prefer to run to the tight-end side rather than the open side because of the Combo Block by the offensive tackle and tight end.

When the fullback gets the handoff, he must roll his stomach over the ball and look to cut off the trap as quickly as possible.

Trap versus a 4-3 run to the tight-end side:

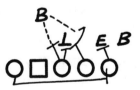

On the trap to the strong side, the tight end must block the defensive end by himself.

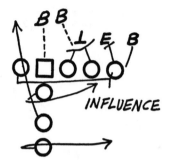

TRAP AGAINST A SPLIT DEFENSE

Again, reduce the front and then run to the reduced front.

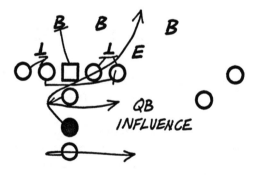

TRAP OPTION (28-27 IN OUR SYSTEM)

The trap option is blocked like the 32-31 trap. The only difference is the offensive guard will trap the outside man against a 50 or odd defense.

If the defense shows a reduced front, the play should be blocked the same as a 32 trap for the sake of simplicity. The offensive guard reads the defensive end. If the defensive end comes in, the guard should bang him and go block the first defensive back.

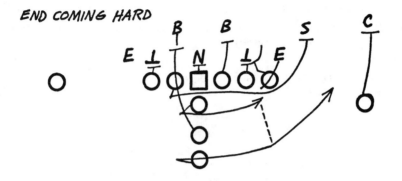

However, 90 percent of the time, the defensive end comes upfield. Now the guard must block the defensive end to the sideline so the pitch man can get inside. If the guard makes this block, you can get a big play.

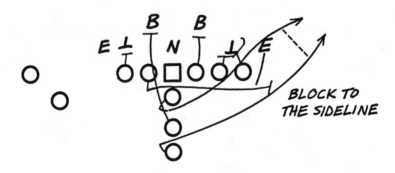

The fullback should get his inside arm up and roll his stomach over the ball. The fullback needs to make a good fake for the play to be successful.

TRAP OPTION AGAINST A 4-3 DEFENSE

The fullback looks for the linebacker. If the fullback makes a good fake, the linebacker should find him. The fullback must keep his neck and head up.

If the defensive end comes in hard, the pulling guard should bang the defensive end and block the defensive back. If the defensive end goes upfield, the guard should trap inside out to the sideline.

The trap option versus a 4-3 defense:

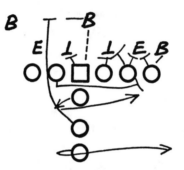

TRAP OPTION AGAINST A SPLIT DEFENSE

We would rather run to the open side against a split or "50" defense. This is because we can pass off the play to the open side to control the defensive secondary. However, we will run the play from anywhere on the field.

Trap option versus a split defense:

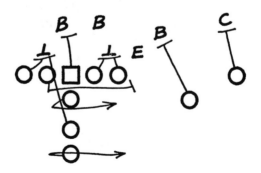

If we throw, we can throw the "one" route or the "two" route or we can pitch the ball. If we throw, the defensive end must be knocked down.

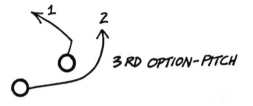

3 RD OPTION-PITCH

POWER PLAY

The power play and blast are our ball-control plays from the "I." The power play is a short-yardage, inside play for the fullback.

If you are going to throw the ball, you had better have something else for a rainy day. The same is true for the option. What will help you is the ability and size of your players. A good offensive front is essential in making the power play effective.

POWER PLAY AGAINST A 5-2

Either a Man Block or a Green Block is used according to game plan. The play should be taught so it utilizes deception.

The fullback rolls over the ball and reads the block on the linebacker. The quarterback brings his hands in quickly and fakes to the "I" back. The "I" back also rolls over the ball and heads into the "three" hole on the other side.

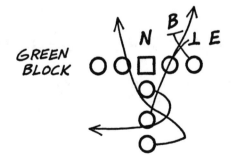

GREEN BLOCK

The quarterback brings his hands in again and runs to the corner while looking at the defensive end.

Against a 5-2, always pick out the weakest linebacker and defensive tackle to run against.

POWER PLAY AGAINST A 4-3

You must decide which side to run to in game plan. Try to get a mismatch of personnel. If the middle linebacker is reading the center, switch block away from the ball on the backside. If the entire defense is tough, "X" Block the play.

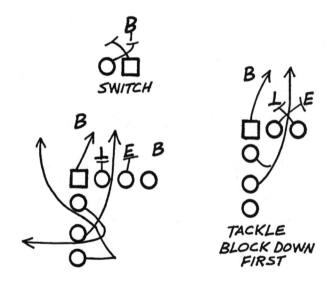

POWER PLAY AGAINST A SPLIT DEFENSE

Reduce the front and run to the reduced front. The fullback reads the linebacker. We Combo Block the defensive tackle and LB.

REDUCED SIDE

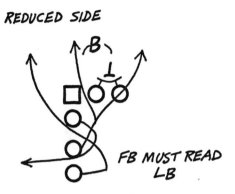

FB MUST READ
LB

DELAY

We use a number and a name to describe the play. The "I" back fakes a step to the right side and comes back. This movement gives misdirection and makes the defense think the play will be blast. We are looking to get a trap at the point of attack.

Your "I" back will become more effective when you begin to give the ball to the fullback, either on misdirection or a read play.

DELAY AGAINST A 5-2 DEFENSE

Our rule is that if we run power to the weakest defensive lineman, we will run delay the other way. The defense cannot keep two linebackers on our "I" back and circle in on him.

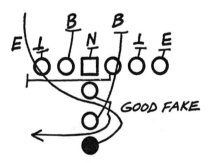

GOOD FAKE

DELAY AGAINST A 4-3 DEFENSE

Run power to the open side and delay to the tight end side to get a double team.

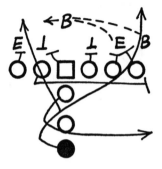

DELAY AGAINST A SPLIT DEFENSE

First, reduce the front. We run delay and power to the same side. If the defense brings a linebacker in, throw the football. Do not run three against four.

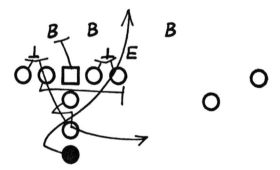

EAGLE STACK

If the defense uses an Eagle Stack, run to the Eagle Stack.

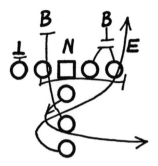

IN CONCLUSION

The "I" formation has been good to us. Some years, our personnel has dictated that we just run blast. Other years, we have used a lot of misdirection with trap option, trap, and delay. Other years, we have used triple option to out-finesse teams.

Our "I" back became much more effective when we started giving the ball to the fullback on a read or misdirection play. The defense cannot keep two linebackers on the "I" back and circle in on him.

DEVELOPING THE TRIPLE OPTION FROM THE "I" AND VEER

To operate from both the "I" and the veer, you must be well organized on the practice field. We coach the triple option every practice, spending seven and one-half minutes in the "I" and seven and one-half minutes in split backs.

TEACHING PROCESS

Start out running the play without a line. Put one pylon where the back is to run and another pylon where the quarterback's first read is. A third pylon should be placed where the second read will be.

TARGET
AREA 1ST READ 2ND READ
□ ○ ○ ○
QB

○ "I" OR SPLIT BACKS
○

QUARTERBACK STEPS

From the "I" formation, the quarterback should take a 45 degree step. In split backs, the quarterback should step right down the line of scrimmage. In either case, the quarterback's feet must have a toe-to-instep relationship for proper balance.

No matter which steps the quarterback uses, his eyes must focus on the read area *immediately.* We have found that this is easier for the quarterback to do from split backs.

The quarterback must decide what to do *before* the dive back is beyond the quarterback's front hip. Deciding *after* is what causes most fumbles. We tell our quarterbacks, if they have not made a decision, *give the dive back the ball.*

The dive back should have his inside arm up and roll over the ball. His outside leg should be to the outside leg of the guard. If the dive back runs to the inside leg, the read area will be diminished. This must be coached every practice. The dive back should have his neck in and head up. He should run to daylight, preferably away from the pursuit. He should get to the sideline as quickly as possible.

The pitch man should be four yards deep by one yard outside (4×1). In the "I" formation, he should not get out too fast. He should be a little lazy and just stay one yard outside.

From split backs, the pitch man must *sprint* to get one yard outside. He should look for the ball on his first step. He must turn his head to the ball and then run.

The quarterback should pitch the ball by sighting with his peripheral vision. This protects him. He can see when he is going to take a hit. (If he cannot see the pitch man, the quarterback should not pitch the ball.) After the pitch, the quarterback should drop his butt and move down to protect himself. We have never had a quarterback hurt pitching the ball at the line of scrimmage.

The quarterback must realize there are several things the defense can do. If the defensive man stays or comes upfield, the quarterback should give the ball to the dive man.

If the defensive man comes down, the quarterback should pull the ball out. Most defensive people will come down to take away the dive.

If the quarterback pulls the ball out, he must then attack the *inside* shoulder of the defensive end. If he attacks the defensive man's outside shoulder, the defensive end will then string the play out.

Walk your quarterbacks through this maneuver. Show them that when the defensive end's shoulder is attacked, he must come on the quarterback or come upfield. Also show your quarterbacks how they will get strung out if they attack the outside shoulder.

We practice this every day except Friday. One day a week we use pylons. The other three days we operate against a defensive front. If you are going to be successful with the option, you must practice it.

In pre-fall practice, we go on the theory that 90 percent of the time we will see one of three defensive fronts—an odd, an even, or a split. We practice the option seven and one-half minutes a day from the "I" and seven and one-half minutes from split backs. We use a half line with a line coach and with a quarterback coach.

One day a week we also work on difficult reads for fifteen minutes. For example, a slant scrape is a difficult read. So is a stack. If we are going to see these defenses, we had better practice against them.

PERIMETER DRILL

We work on option and play-action passes during this time. This drill teaches receivers to block and also teaches the defensive secondary to come up and play against the run. The receivers are blocking the defensive secondary. The perimeter drill is live except for the quarterback. This drill will be discussed later in further detail in Chapter 11, "Implementing an Effective Team Offense."

First drill diagram:

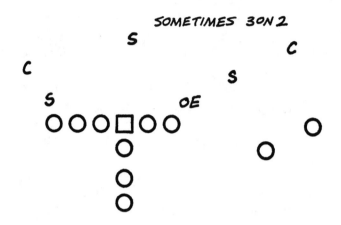

Second drill diagram:

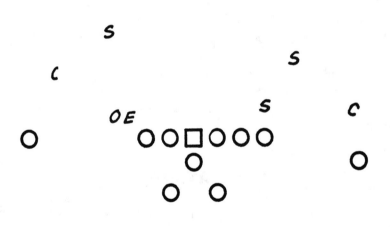

OUTSIDE VEER

The outside veer is the best short-yardage and goal-line play there is, although it can also be effective in the middle of the field. The play has averaged 5.7 yards a carry for us.

The outside veer is one of the reasons why we run a multiple set ("I" and split backs) offense. The outside veer is not as effective from the "I" as from split backs because it doesn't attack the target area fast enough.

The two plays we prefer to run from split backs are the outside-veer and lead-option pass or run.

On the outside veer, the dive back runs a path of his inside leg to the outside leg of the defensive tackle.

SAME-PATH THEORY

The University of Houston tried to run the inside and outside veer on the same path for simplicity in teaching. We tried this for a year and found it hurt our outside veer play. We got clogged up inside and didn't get the quarterback to the corner as well. Possibly, we weren't coaching this right. However, the year we tried it, our outside veer average went down to 3.4 yards per play.

Diagram of the Same-Path Theory:

INSIDE LEG OF
THE TACKLE

TEACHING POINT

The quarterback must be familiar with two reads. The first read is the defensive end. The second read is the defensive back. If run correctly, the outside veer will result in a three-on-two situation. There must be a seal inside. We prefer to run the play to the tight end side.

The dive back must run the correct path to get us close to the double-team block. When we were running the path of the inside veer, we weren't able to put as much pressure on the linebackers or get as close to that double-team block.

The outside veer should be coached for ten minutes every day. The outside veer:

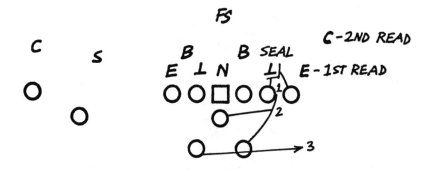

QUARTERBACK STRAIGHT DOWN THE LINE

After receiving the snap, the quarterback should go straight down the line of scrimmage. He first must pivot and not get overextended. The correct relationship of his feet is toe-to-instep. Usually, the quarterback will have to make a decision on his fourth step. If he is 6'-3", he will not need as many steps. If he is 5'-7", he will probably need more steps.

Once the quarterback gets to the read area, he should be under control. The quarterback should not slow up the dive back.

Outside Veer-Blocking against a 5-2

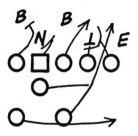

Outside Veer-Blocking against an Even

Because of the end Jam Technique, the tight end may have to release outside.

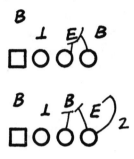

Outside Veer-Blocking against a Split Defense

Diagram:

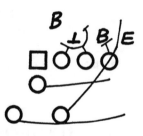

Outside Veer-Blocking against a 6-5 Wide Defense

Diagram:

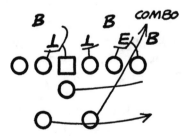

TEACHING PROCESS

When we teach outside veer-blocking, our quarterbacks are the reads, not our coaches. This allows our quarterbacks to get a feel for what the defensive ends and defensive backs can do. It also helps them see how the play can be read.

First, the quarterbacks work with two reads. Then the play is half-line blocked. In pre-fall, we go over every defensive set there is. During the season we prepare for certain sets according to game plan.

ADAPTING

If the defense overloads to stop the outside veer, run triple option back away from it. To make the defense play an honest base front (down linemen and linebackers), you will need an effective audible system.

The defense can stop the outside veer and it can stop the triple option (inside veer). But it cannot stop both unless you don't execute or you are very, very inferior physically.

There will still be secondary people coming hard to the alleys. That is why you will also need to be able to execute the triple-option pass or run.

OPTION BASE AND OPTION PITCH

Option base and option pitch should be taught only in your feeder system to familiarize your players with the fundamentals of the option. Coaches have gotten out of option football because they just run base and pitch. When you only do base and pitch, you are getting away from option football.

When we teach base, our freshmen quarterbacks do only base the first couple of days (or up to two weeks depending on the quarterback). Then the quarterback gets in and starts reading defenses.

In base, you must block the first read. The fullback runs the same path as in the triple option and the tailback stays 4×1.

When the ball is pitched, your team had better be able to block the defense.

If you are running base, you are playing power football. We feel the intent of option football is to *out finesse* people. In offensive football today, you must be a read team. If not, you had better have the size to run a three-yards and a cloud-of-dust offense.

When I coached at the high school level, we ran option base and pitch in the seventh and eighth grades. In the ninth grade, we ran read. I disagree with any high school coaching philosophy that says a player will not be able to read the option or the secondary. If you have direction in your teaching process, option or secondary reads can be taught effectively.

FUMBLES

Again, if you run the option package, you are going to fumble the ball now and then. You must be able to live with this. Coach so you don't fumble *too* much—but you are still going to fumble some.

7

TEACHING THE
VEER OFFENSE

LEAD OPTION

Some people call the lead option the speed option. It is an effective play against a hard defensive end.
  A hard defensive end:

  The lead option also serves to protect your quarterback and allows you to get the ball outside.

LEAD OPTION LINE-BLOCKING

When going to the right, the quarterback should first step back with his left foot. He then steps back with his right foot. He must turn his hips so he can run to the inside shoulder of the defensive end. The quarterback's eyes must be on the defensive end.

The quarterback should pitch the ball at a distance where the defensive end cannot fake and come upfield on the pitch man. He must not pitch the ball too early. After pitching the ball, the quarterback must drop his hips and protect himself.

LEAD BACK BLOCK

The lead back blocker should take three steps laterally and read the secondary contain. He must then go immediately to block the contain. The lead back blocker should not block until he steps on the contain man's toes. He must go to the defensive man quickly so the inside pursuit cannot get to the ball.

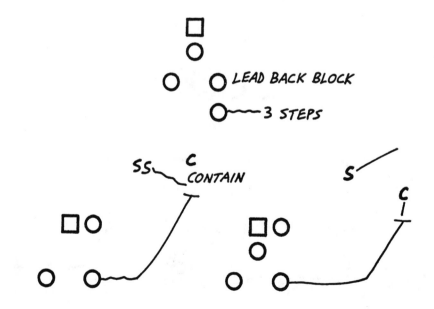

We teach two techniques for the lead back block. One is to block the outside knee of the contain man. The other is to stick the face mask into the sternum area of the defender. The blocker should then "rip up" with his forearms and bring his hips with him.

OUTSIDE RECEIVER BLOCK

The outside receiver blocks the deep secondary man.

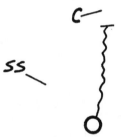

The outside receiver should come off the line hard as if the play were going to be a pass. The receiver should create a cushion. He should start his block when he can step on the defensive back's toes. He should stick his face mask into the defender's sternum, "rip up" with his forearms, and bring his hips right through the man.

PITCH MAN TECHNIQUE

The pitch man must look for the ball on his first step. After receiving the ball, he should stay on the outside hip of the lead back as long as possible. This will allow him to get the ball outside away from pursuit.

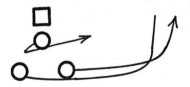

We like to run the play from the wide-slot and pro formations.
Wide slot:

Pro set:

The lead option:

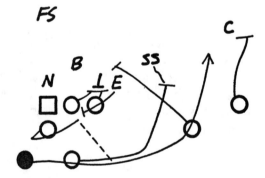

To stop the lead option, defenses went to three-on-two
coverage.

C   Fs
           S   c

E
O O O □ O O   O
                O

Offenses then began to key the free safety at the line of scrimmage. If the play is run to the tight end side, the tight end must get a good seal at the line of scrimmage.

If the free safety lines up on the center, the play should be run to the "two" receiver side. If opposite, it should be run to the tight end side. Remember, we are talking about the play being run from the wide-slot formation.

When teams started getting the safety man to the alley, it was important to come up with an adjustment. Thus, the lead option was combined with the quick-passing game to create a softer cushion in the secondary.

LOADED OPTION

The loaded option protects the quarterback, gets the quarterback into the secondary, and allows the pitch upfield. Everything is run the same as in the outside veer. Every coaching point is the same *except* the lead back will block the defensive end. All defensive fronts are blocked the same as the outside veer except the back blocks the read area on the line of scrimmage.

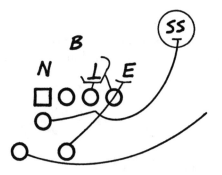

ADJUSTMENTS

Two adjustments can be made. If you double team "two," read "three."

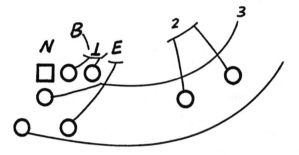

If you double team "three," read "two."

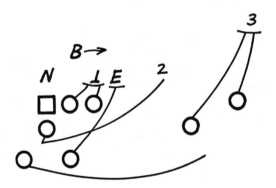

The weakness of this is the playside linebacker. You must get the offensive tackle on him to seal him. This is a difficult block.

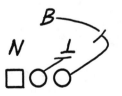

THE PITCH

If you get the pitch upfield, you can get a big play. The quarterback does not have to have 4.6 speed in the 40-yard dash. If he is 4.8 or 4.9, he can get upfield to make the pitch.

COUNTER OPTION

Against a 5-2 defense, the guard has to fire out straight at the linebacker. The quarterback takes two steps and reverse pivots. The play should be ball-faked. On the mesh, the quarterback should be looking at the defensive end. If he does not see the defensive end, there is a great chance of his getting injured.

The guard has a straight-ahead block. The dive back runs to the inside hip of the offensive guard. The quarterback pivots and reads on the defensive end. The other back takes one false step in the opposite direction and then pivots to get 4×1.

On the 32 counter, give the ball to the dive back. On 28 counter option, option the end. You cannot run counter option without running counter dive.

The counter option can result in a big play if people are pursuing the option and trying to string it out. It is easier to get the linebackers to step in one direction and then seal them. With the defense pursuing hard and defensive backs coming hard to the alleys, misdirection can create a big play.

Run to the short side if the defense is protecting the wide side three-on-two.

Counter Option:

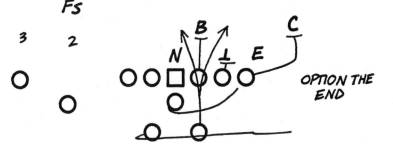

Counter Dive:

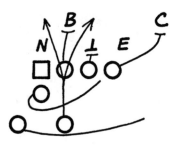

It is important that the step in misdirection be taken. The guard must come out on the linebacker. The backer must be held with the fake. It should be decided in game plan what you are going to do with the corner, block him or read him.

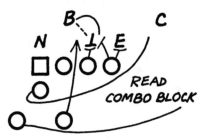

AUDIBLE PHILOSOPHY

If the defensive front is unbalanced, we will run away from the strength. If the front and secondary are both unbalanced, we will run to the unbalanced secondary. If there is a balanced front and an unbalanced secondary, we will run away from the unbalanced secondary. Our audible system will be discussed in greater detail in Chapter 10, "Training the Option Quarterback."

No matter what you run, you must attack the perimeter by first sealing inside. Again, misdirection helps seal because defensive players are trying to string things out and get to the alleys to stop your basic plays—the inside veer (triple option) and outside veer. You must have a misdirection play off every main play you run.

CRAZY OPTION

This is a form of a misdirection play. You want the defense to think you are running inside veer. The quarterback should have a toe-to-instep relationship with his feet for a solid base and body control. The quarterback should make a fake pivot, come back and attack the inside shoulder of the defensive end. The guard will have to pull to protect the quarterback.

The dive back runs the inside veer (triple option) path. There must be a good fake. The pitch man takes two steps to the center area and comes back hard to get a 4×1 relationship.

The crazy option is blocked like the trap option. The guard blocks down on the defensive end, bangs him, and blocks "two." If the defensive end is upfield, the guard blocks him to the sideline. This will allow the pitch.

The crazy option is effective because the defense is trying to take away the triple option. If the quarterback has 4.8 or 4.9 speed in the 40-yard dash, the play might gain fifteen yards. If the quarterback has 4.6 speed, the play might result in a touchdown.

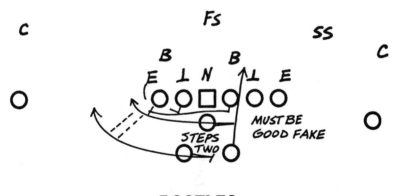

BOOTLEG

The main reason to run bootleg is to get misdirection. We usually run the bootleg off option or inside veer, off blast, and off delay. We generally won't run bootleg off all three in one game. This is decided in game plan. If we plan to run option, we will run option bootleg. If we plan to control the ball, we may use blast bootleg. If our opponents pursue well, we will probably run delay and option bootleg.

We will run bootleg out of the "I" or split backs. We are trying to get a two-on-one situation in the corner zone. If the corner is deep, the quarterback should throw to the tight end. If the corner rolls up, the quarterback should throw to the flanker deep. The guard must get depth and block the man in contain. A fake to the dive back helps the guard get to the defensive end.

BLAST BOOTLEG

To execute the blast bootleg, the quarterback pulls the ball in and reverses to get depth. His head should be over his shoulder so he can look downfield to see what is happening.

The dive back goes to the middle third area on a delay type of route. The pitch man blocks the end on the backside to prevent a backside rush. Which corner we want to attack will be decided in game plan.

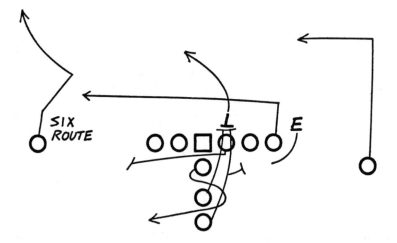

DELAY BOOTLEG

In the delay bootleg, the quarterback makes two fakes.

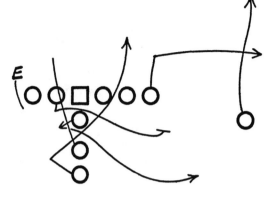

OPTION BOOTLEG

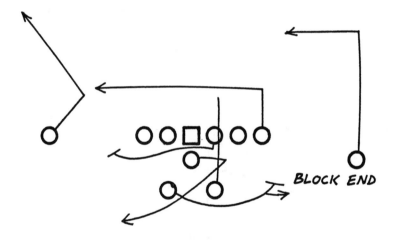

If the defense has three-on-two coverage, we prefer to run bootleg back to the tight end side out of the wide-slot formation.

The things that make the bootleg go are good fakes and good execution. The quarterback must get depth. His fakes should get him outside. We tell the guard to block the defensive end.

We will run the same bootleg from different formations. This is decided in game plan by what we are trying to do in the defensive secondary

INSIDE GAME

Windback

The windback, covered in Chapter 5, "Coaching the "I" Formation Running Game," can also be run from the veer. It can result in a big play because defenses are thinking option and trying to get out and stop the perimeter.

The linebacker must be moved so the back can wind back when he gets to the target area at the line of scrimmage. The defensive tackle must be blocked. We use the Switch Block. The center takes the defensive tackle to create an alley. The back must read the middle linebacker because the play might not end up as a windback. It could be a dive if the linebacker steps up and reads the center. However, this does not happen very often.

When the quarterback gives the back the ball, he must get his hands to the far hip to get deception. This is very important.

Windback versus a 4-3 Defense

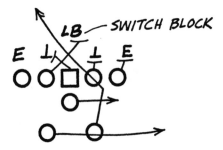

Windback against a Split

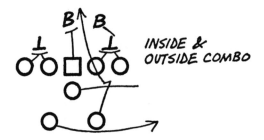

If the linebacker steps inside, read the linebacker and don't wind it back.

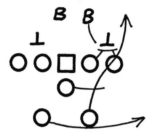

Windback versus a 5-2 Defense

The main change is in the path of the dive back. His path is more inside.

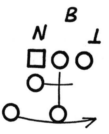

The dive back cuts off the block on the nose guard.

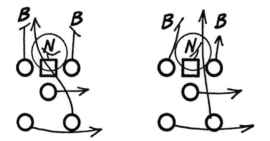

8

INCORPORATING THE OPTION PACKAGE PASSING GAME

THE QUICK-PASSING GAME

To stop the option, defensive coaches began putting one man on the quarterback, one man on the dive back, and one man on the pitch man. They also began sending a defender to the alley. This made the receiver's block more difficult. It also made it more difficult to run the football against nine- and ten-man fronts.

Depending on what the defense was doing in the secondary, we were concerned about two defenders rolling up or the free safety coming to the alley.

We had to protect the quarterback, so we incorporated the quick passing game off lead option with the pass-first, pitch-second philosophy.

When we first began teaching this, we gave the quarterback only three options. We ran designated routes and tried not to give the quarterback too much to handle at once. His three options were: to throw to one receiver; to throw to another receiver; or to pitch the ball. We also wanted an option we could audible to.

If 41 was called, the split end ran 82. If 42 was called, the split end ran 81.

The quarterback was to take two steps back before he came down the line of scrimmage. If the 81 route was open, he was to throw the ball. If it was not open, he was to look to 42. If the 42 route was not open, the quarterback was to pitch the ball.

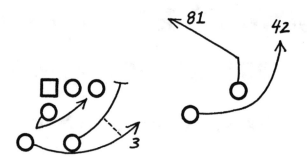

This was good to us. Defenses came up and thought we were in lead option. The play held the defensive secondary. However, we found that when we had one route called, we should have had another route called because of the different secondary coverages.

The following spring, we found that we could key the corner with 81-82 read. If the corner went back, we could throw in the seam.

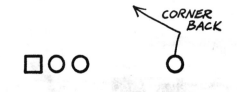

If the corner rolled up, we could throw the fade pattern.

The second receiver was running a designated route on 81-82 read.

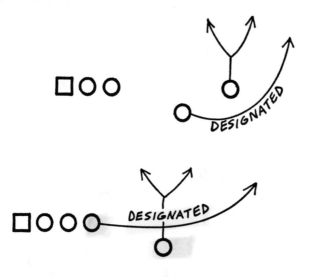

BASKETBALL COVERAGE

We found that both the receiver and the quarterback could read the corner. Teams then began to defense us with inside-outside or Basketball Coverage.

We had to come up with a play against Basketball Coverage. The play was 81 and 81 Go. What we were now doing was packaging routes—giving our receivers two routes to run depending on what the secondary did. If the safety came in, we threw over his head on the 81 Go pattern.

81 Go:

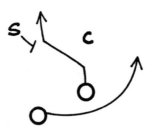

MOTION

The next area of concern was what to do if we were in motion. If the "two" man covered the motion man, we used the "one" route.

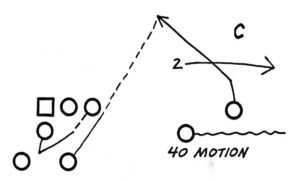

If the corner covered the motion, we tried to throw the "two" route.

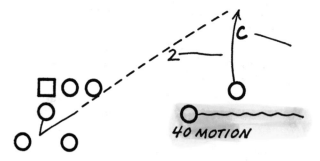

If the defense gave us Basketball Coverage (inside-outside), we ran the "1" Go and Double 2 routes.

"1" Go Route:

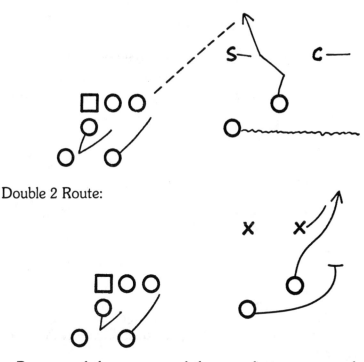

Double 2 Route:

Because of the success of the pass-first, run-second option, defenses started to play us three-on-two. We now had to come up with something to keep the free safety at home. We decided to shift our tight end back out of a pro set and use a double split with the tight end in the slot. If the free safety stayed three-on-two, we would audible to the one-on-one principle.

One-on-one principle:

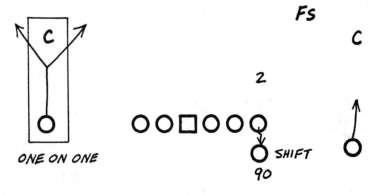

THE PITCH

We also felt we had to open an alley for the pitch. When we ran a 50 motion play, defenses brought a man across. We then had a one-on-one situation with our split end. This also opened an alley for the option.

Defenses then began to play four across against the 50 motion. When they did this, we had a two-on-two situation on the other side, plus the pitch.

Two-on-two, plus the pitch:

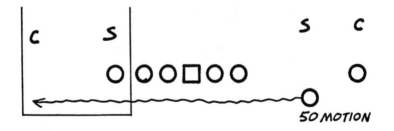

When we used the 50 motion, we got a one-on-one situation with the "one" route. We could move the ball, but we wanted a controlled pass to the outside. This was because much of the time our split end was taking a lot of punishment. Therefore, we went to an 82-83 or 42-43 read. Now, we could throw the ball without waiting for the receiver to hitch. This was a good third-down play for down and distance.

If the corner was in deep cushion, the receiver would run the "three" route.

The 83 read:

If the corner rolled up or the receiver felt he could beat the corner deep, the receiver would run the "two" route.

The "two" route:

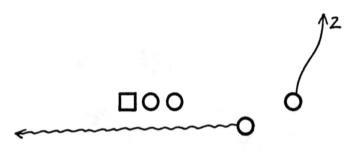

PLAY-ACTION PASSING GAME

If you are going to throw the play-action pass, you must do it off your best running play to make the secondary react. Our play-action passes are the option 3 and 4 pass, the counter-option pass, the trap-option pass, and the option bootleg pass.

Option 3 and 4 Pass

If the corner rolls, throw the "two" route to try to beat the secondary rotation in the open spot.

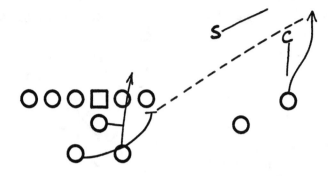

If the coverage is a two-on-two Basketball (inside-outside), run option four pass with an 81 Go route. Make the safety think you are going to run the "one" route and then just go upfield.

Option 4 pass, 81 Go route:

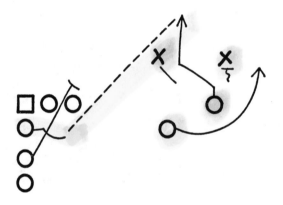

If the strong safety comes up hard, throw the "one" route (41).

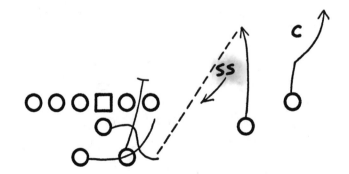

If the free safety is coming to the option, there will be a one-on-one situation to the other side. We will run a 94 post with the tight end going to the area the free safety left. It helps if the tight end has 4.8 or 4.7 speed in the 40-yard dash.

The 94 post:

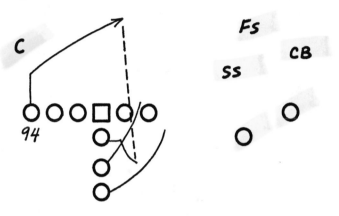

COUNTER-OPTION PASS

If you run the option package, you must run counter option. We prefer to run it to the "two" receiver side because we have three options instead of two.

When the quarterback reverses, he ball fakes. The guard pulls and gets in the defensive end's face. The quarterback must run to at least the tackle area to put pressure on the strong safety or defensive cornerback.

The counter-option gets the secondary stepping in the opposite direction. This will help you seal inside.

Counter-option pass:

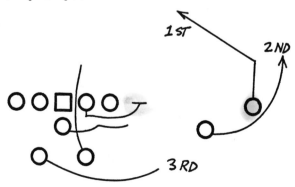

TRAP-OPTION PASS

For us, the trap-option pass is a tight end pass against three-on-two coverage. If we wish to run to the other side, we will run the quick-passing game.

The guard must block the defensive end. He must knock the defensive end inside-out to the sideline.

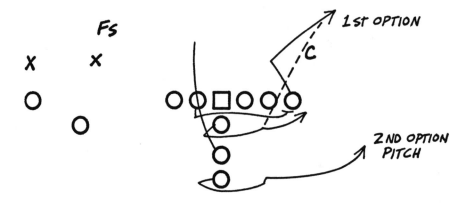

OPTION BOOTLEG

Our fourth play action pass is the option bootleg.

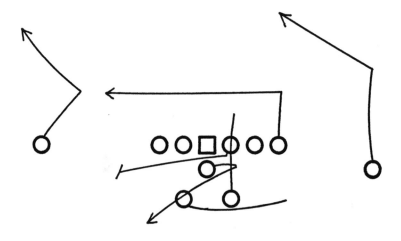

THE SPRINT-OUT PASSING GAME

We want to use minimum routes in the sprint-out passing game. The routes should be good precision routes. There should be a designated route against any coverage possible. You do not need a lot of patterns as long as you have a plan. Execution and reading the secondary are very important. Once again, we name our sprint-out routes. We number our quick-passing game and play action routes.

SPRINT-OUT GAME READS

Reading the secondary is crucial. We believe we can get a pre-snap read on two-on-two, three-on-two, and Two Deep, Five Under Coverage.

If the defense is disguising its coverages by stemming up and back, run motion the minute the defense stems. *The best way to get a pre-snap read is to run motion.*

QUARTERBACK STEPS

On the three-step sprint out, the ball should be thrown when the quarterback's foot hits on the third step. The quarterback should plant his inside leg and snap his head.

On the three-step out or slant to the left, the quarterback's first step should be with his left foot. On his second step, he must hop around, stand tall, and throw the ball. The hop will enable him to square up to the target.

On the five-step sprint out, the quarterback should hop on his fourth step. On the seven-step sprint out, the quarterback should hop on his sixth step.

Throw your short routes when you get a big cushion. On the four-yard out, the catch point is going to be about seven or eight yards. The quarterback will use the three-step sprint out.

The five-step sprint out is for medium routes. The seven-step sprint out is for deeper routes. You must work on this every day.

If you are going to throw long, you must practice it. If you are going to throw short, you must practice it.

DOUBLE BLOCK ON THE CORNER

On the Double-Team Block, your fullback and running back must go out and block the defensive end on the other side or in the neutral zone. The fullback should stick his face mask into the inside breast of the defensive end. He should try to step on the defensive end's toes so he doesn't start too early.

The "I" back should hit the outside breast of the defensive end. He must sprint to do this. The fullback and "I" back should hit the defensive end at the same time or very close to the same time.

After the fullback and "I" back have made contact, they should turn their hips inside and get butt-to-butt.

This block is also called the Control Block.

CUT BLOCK

In college, you are still allowed to block below the waist on the defensive end. The fullback should block the inside knee of the defensive end with his face mask. The "I" back blocks the outside knee of the defensive end. Both the fullback and "I" back must keep their necks and heads up. They should hit together or bang-bang. When they hit, they should try to get their buttocks together. If the opponent is not knocked down, they must scramble.

We work on this block five to ten minutes every practice. This is an EDD—an Every Day Drill.

SWING ROUTE

This pattern is used against Invert or Sky Coverage. We key the corner, though some teams will key the strong safety. The split end runs a curl pattern of up to twelve yards. The split end should be in the seam so the opposing inside linebacker cannot cover him.

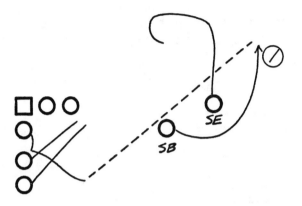

The Swing Route is also a good pattern against man-to-man coverage. The main receiver is now the slot back. (Remember, we key the cornerback. He will tell us the coverage.)

BENCH PATTERN

Against corner roll or Cloud Coverage, throw to the split end. The pattern is called Bench in our system.
Bench Pattern:

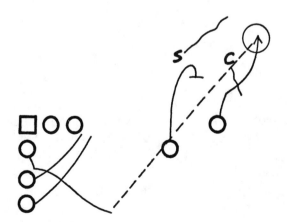

CROSS PATTERN

This pattern is used against man coverage. By crossing the receivers, you can get a running pick and usually free one of the two receivers.

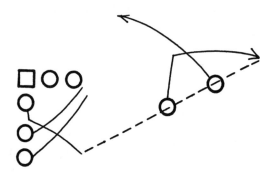

If the linebackers are stunting inside, slant the split end inside and throw to the slot back in the flat.

SEAM PATTERN

We use this pattern against Two-on-Two Deep, Five Under Coverage. Double block on the corner. The fullback slides off into the flat. If the defensive end drops off, the fullback should bang him and release to the open spot. If the defensive end runs with the fullback, the fullback should plant and come underneath. You are trying to get two receivers in the safety area. Consider the safety a corner

Seam Pattern:

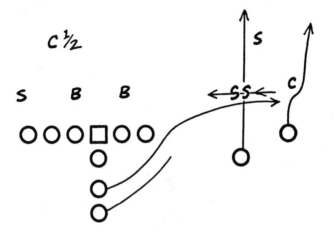

THREE-ON-TWO

If we get a three-on-two by the defense against our sprint-out game, we will go to a double split with the tight end. We will shift the tight end out wide.

We can also shift the tight end out of the pro set.

If the defense does not make an adjustment after we shift, we will run a 94 read. The quarterback takes a five-step sprint out and passes to the tight end.

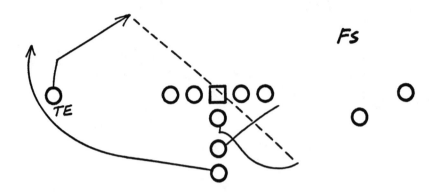

If the defense plays us inside out, we will use a 92 read call. The split end calls either the tailback's name "Tom" or his number "24." The tailback comes on a throwback route. We do this any time the defense brings the end out or we run sprint draw and wind it back. With these two reads, the free safety must stay at home. There is no way the defense will be able to play us three-on-two. When the free safety adjusts, we will then go back to our two-on-two principle.

OUT PATTERN

If the strong safety takes the out away with quick flat rotation, throw to the slot back on a curl.

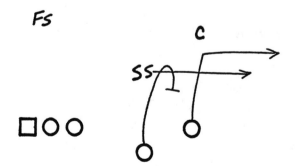

If the strong safety is playing curl-to-flat, the out is open.

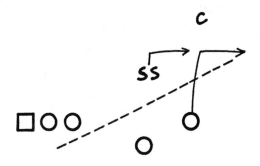

A wide split end from the slot will control the fast flat coverage by the strong safety.

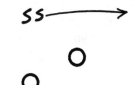

If the corner rolls up to take away the out, throw to the slot back.

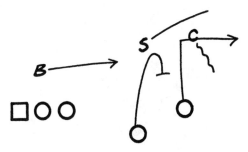

POST PATTERN

We call any Post Pattern "four" whether it be 94 (tight end), 84 (split end), or 44 (slot back). In a one-back offense, we could also use 24.

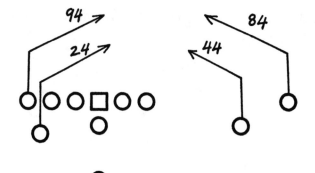

POST CORNER

The quarterback must read the defensive corner. The defensive back should think the receiver is running a post route. The receiver must "sell the post" for the Post Corner to be successful. We have 86, 46, and 96 Post Corner routes. We also have a 26 route from the one-back offense.

The 86 route:

In the 26 route, the 80 man must come under the 20 man. The 26 route:

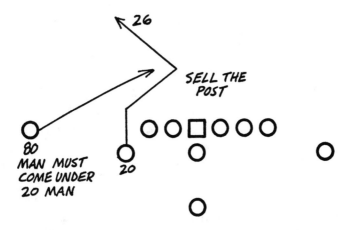

QUARTERBACK READS

Your quarterbacks must be able to read two-on-two, three-on-two, Two Deep and Three Deep Coverages on the pre-snap and post-snap read. They must understand that 99 percent of the time when the defense is three-on-two, they bring the corner to the flat. This is called Cloud or Corner Roll Coverage. Your quarterbacks must be able to read Cloud Coverage so they don't force the ball. They must take what the defense gives.

Cloud Coverage:

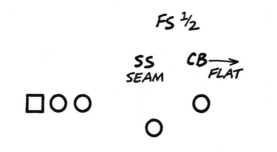

Your quarterbacks must also understand that if the strong safety rotates to the flat, the coverage is Invert or Sky.

Sky Coverage:

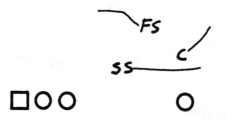

Do not allow the defense to play you three-on-two. Shift or run motion to prevent this.

If the defense is in Man Coverage, it can play you in two ways. It can go where you go or it can play you outside-inside (Basketball Coverage).

Basketball Coverage:

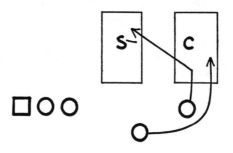

If the defense is two-on-two, you can beat that coverage if you execute.

If the coverage is three-on-two, do not throw against it. Get the defense out of three-on-two by splitting the tight end or by motion. Someone has to cover the motion.

TWO DEEP, FIVE UNDER ZONE

If the defense is Two Deep, Five Under Zone, it will probably give you a pre-snap read by alignment. If the defense disguises it, you will have problems. Therefore, you must run motion to get a pre-snap read. When the defense is Five Under, Two Deep Zone, it has won the war in the short zones. You should try to run the slot back and split end deep and get the ball there.

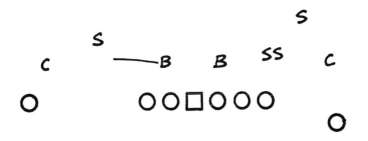

TWO DEEP, FIVE UNDER MAN

If the defense plays Two Deep, Five Under Man, their linebackers will be forced to take your backs man for man. First, run option because the defense has no one out there for contain. If it is a definite passing situation, throw to the back coming out of the backfield.

FIVE DEFENSIVE BACKS (NICKEL) COVERAGES

The recent emphasis on the pass has brought about more use of Nickel Defenses. The defensive people are three by three—three yards out from the tight end and three yards off the ball, three yards off the quick tackle and three yards off the ball, etc.

There are three types of Nickel Defenses.

First Type of Nickel Defense

In the first type, the defense has taken away the one-on-one with the split end and forced the offense to attack two-on-two.

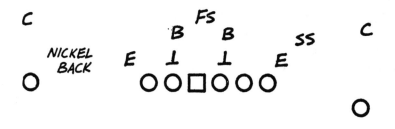

If the defense is a true three deep, get the ball upfield and attack the seams. We try to coach either the one-on-one or the two-on-two. We also use motion from the wide out or from the backs. We will get two-on-two or three-on-two until the defense adjusts. The defense will have to drop the end or bring a backer or the free safety into that zone.

The use of five defensive backs has created more back motion and brought in shifting formations, for example quickside trips, to get four receivers out quickly.

Teams are almost forcing you to run the ball inside with the first type of five-defensive-back alignment. The optional screen will attack this type of defense.

Second Type of Nickel Defense

The second type of five-defensive-back coverage is Man Coverage with bump-and-run on the outside receivers. When the defense does this, throw underneath to your backs or throw to your tight end. If the defense is a zone, throw in the seams to your outside receivers.

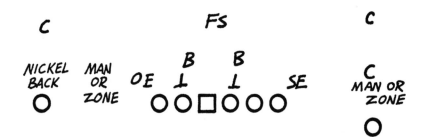

Third Type of Nickel Coverage

Use the same concept against the third type of five-defensive-back coverage. If the defense has a man on the outside receiver and the tight end, throw to your backs. If the defense plays zone outside, try to throw in the seam. Some coaches will also play Nickel Coverage with a two-deep philosophy.

The two-deep philosophy:

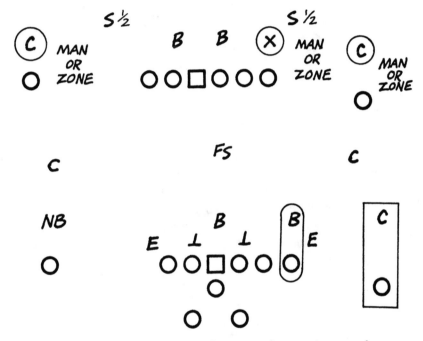

If the defense doubles on the outside receiver and uses a bump-and-run, we tell the receiver to go deep. We then throw underneath.

If the defense bumps and zones outside, we tell our receivers to run the Square-in Route to get into the seams. The outside receivers must read this as they come off the ball into their patterns.

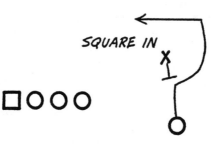

USE MOTION

Use motion if the secondary is disguising its coverages by stemming. When we run motion, we will have a pre-snap read. If the defense ignores the motion, throw to the motion man. If the defense adjusts, take what it gives you.

Motion also changes formations and forces the secondary to adjust. Then take what the secondary gives whether it be one-on-one, two-on-two, or three-on-three. Take what will be your best percentage play.

BACKFIELD MOTION

20 Motion—Right or Left

The 20 motion is motion by our running back, either right or left.

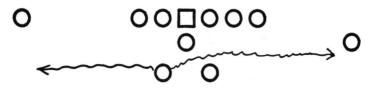

30 Motion—Right or Left

The 30 motion is motion by our fullback, right or left.

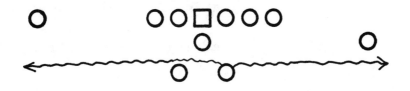

These two types of motion will give you four receivers. The defense must then give you a pre-snap read. You will force the defense to five defensive backs with motion. Most teams will bring one linebacker outside. If the defense does this, run the quarterback draw or trap inside with the other back.

Receiver Motion

Receiver motion will open up an alley or a seam. If the defense does not replace the alley or seam, you can run or throw there effectively.

40 Motion

The 40 motion is motion by the slot back to the split end side.

50 Motion

The 50 motion is motion by the slot back toward the tight end. Therefore, the formation will shift from a slot to a pro set.

60 Motion

The 60 motion is motion by the flanker to the slot. The formation will then shift from a pro to a slot.

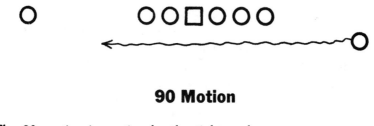

90 Motion

The 90 motion is motion by the tight end.

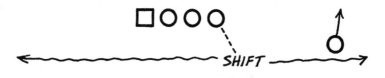

OPTION PACKAGE PASSING GAME REVIEW

The quick-passing game is off option action and has to happen bang-bang, right now. The sprint-out passing game takes advantage of certain coverages. The routes are deeper than in the quick-passing game but might not go for as much yardage. You must have backside reads in the sprint-out game or the defense will play you three-on-two. The sprint draw is a useful running play when the defense is looking for the pass.

The sprint draw:

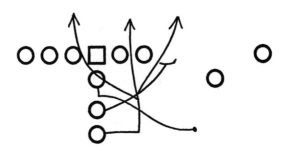

COACHING THE
SPLIT RECEIVERS

A split receiver must have mental discipline. He must have complete concentration on the ball. He must *look the ball in by putting his nose and eyes to the ball.*

After catching the ball, the receiver *must tuck the ball away.* In practice, we overexaggerate tucking the ball away.

On a ball caught below the belt, the receiver's little fingers should be together. On a ball caught above the waist, the receiver's thumbs should be together.

On a ball caught over the shoulder, we prefer that the receiver's thumbs be out. If a receiver comes to us who has always caught the ball over his shoulder with his thumbs in, we will allow him to continue catching the ball in such a manner—if he is effective.

A receiver should try to catch the ball at its highest point. If the pass pattern designates, he should step back to the ball instead of waiting for the ball to come to him.

A receiver should have handling-the-ball drills. He should bounce the ball on the ground and catch it. He should also practice bringing the ball through his legs, around his waist, and around his shoulders.

READING COVERAGES

Because of the increased use of read routes, it is very important that receivers understand secondary coverages. An intelligent receiver will be a better receiver than one who just runs his routes. You must teach your receivers the types of coverages and the open areas in those coverages.

There are eight basic coverages utilized at the present time. The open areas that the receivers must be aware of and be able to get to are circled in the diagrams below.

Invert Rotation Cover Three

Invert Rotation Cover Three is also called "Sky." The strong safety rotates to the flat.

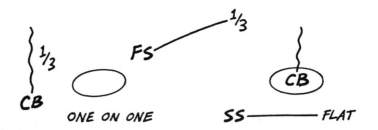

Corner Roll Cover Three

Corner Roll Cover Three is also called "Cloud" coverage.

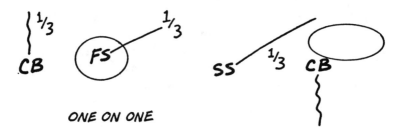

Cover Two, Five Under Man

The third coverage we see is Cover Two, Five Under Man. The flat area is open throwing by the quarterback to a back. The tight end should also be open underneath. In addition, it is difficult to cover the option with Cover Two, Five Under Man because there is no one out there for contain.

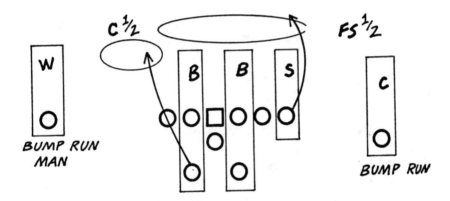

Cover Two, Five Under Zone

The fourth coverage we see is Cover Two, Five Under Zone.

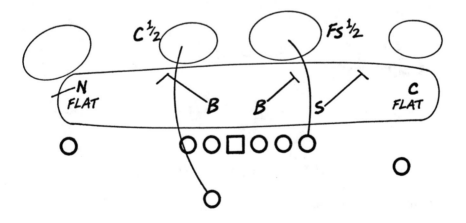

Nickel Defense, Three Deep

The fifth coverage is Nickel Three Deep.

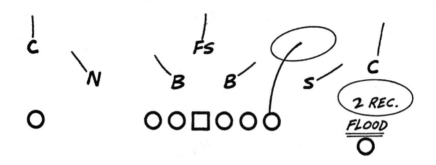

Nickel Defense, Man or Zone Under

Against this defense, you can throw to your backs on a flood pattern or a screen. You can also throw underneath to your tight end. If the defense is Man Under, you can also run the option since there will be no one in contain.

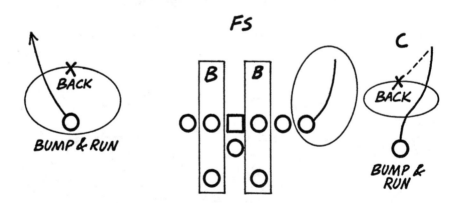

Nickel Defense, Four Under Zone

Against this coverage, attack in the seams.

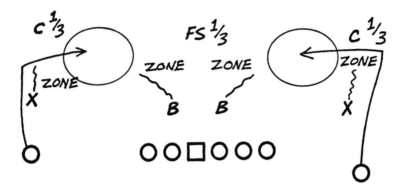

Nickel Defense, One Linebacker Inside

This defense has one linebacker inside with the other linebacker covering the tight end. The defense can be either Man Under or Zone Under. If the defense is Man Under, run the option, throw to the backs on flood patterns, or use screens.

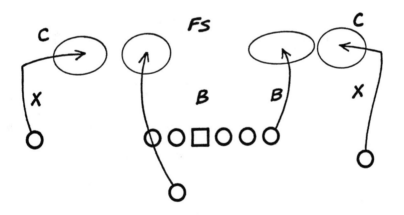

DROP-BACK AND PLAY-ACTION ROUTES

Our drop-back and play-action routes are numbered. We have a passing tree which we work on daily. This passing tree consists of seven patterns. Number one is a slant route. If upfield, the route is "l" Go. Number two is a fade route. Number three is a hitch route. Number four is a post route. Number five is a drag route. Number six is a post corner. Number seven is a curl. Passing Tree:

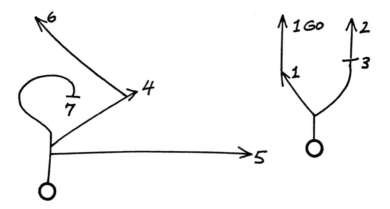

SPRINT-OUT GAME ROUTES

Our sprint-out routes are named. These routes are covered in Chapter 8, "Incorporating the Option Package Passing Game."

WIDE RECEIVER BLOCKS

Wide receiver blocks are very important to the option football team. Your receivers must be able to execute the Control Block, the Crack-Back Block, and the Cut-Off Block.

Control Block

To execute the Control Block, the receiver must come off the line of scrimmage at full speed until he is close enough to step on the cornerback's toes. The receiver should then break down and stick his face mask into the defender's sternum. The receiver should bring his hips right through the man. It is very important that he does not lunge at the cornerback. The receiver must keep his buttocks and legs under him. He must also stay in front of the cornerback and the ball carrier. It is the responsibility of the ball carrier to cut off the receiver's block.

Crack-Back Block

The receiver must move immediately at the defensive back. He should then stick his face mask into the chest area of the defensive back. The receiver should not hit the defensive back in the back. He should be patient and wait for the defensive back to turn and face him. The receiver must not let the defensive back break the seam.

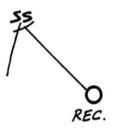

Cut-Off Block

The receiver *must* step in the direction of the ball. He should not step at the defensive back. He should stick his face mask on the inside chest area of the defender and turn his buttocks upfield. The receiver should block for six seconds. To take advantage of the Cut-Off Block, the receiver must know where the ball is going.

10

TRAINING THE
OPTION QUARTERBACK

It is very important that your quarterbacks understand up-to-date defensive fronts as well as current pass coverages. Usually, your quarterbacks will be looking at a seven- or an eight-man front. Because of Nickel Pass Coverages, your quarterbacks will sometimes see a five- or a six-man front. If you are an option team, you will probably not be seeing many six-man fronts except in obvious passing situations.

Ninety percent of the time, the defense will be in one of three fronts—an Even, an Odd, or a Split.

EVEN DEFENSES

We tell our quarterbacks that an Even Defense is an even number of people on the line of scrimmage. There could be four people on the line of scrimmage or there could be six. Some call the 4-3 Defense a 6-1.

We flip-flop our offensive line to try to get our best blockers on the opponent's weakest players. Against the Even Front, we would rather run outside veer to the tight end side and inside veer to the open side depending upon coverages.

The two main Even Defenses are the 4-3 College and the 4-3 Pro.

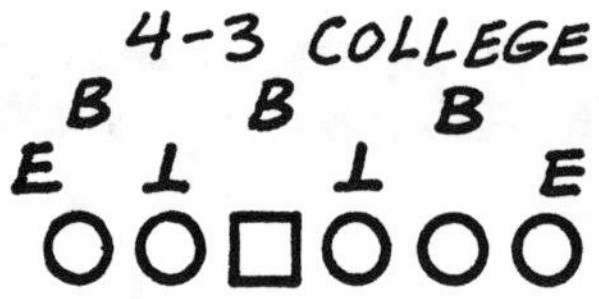

4-3 COLLEGE

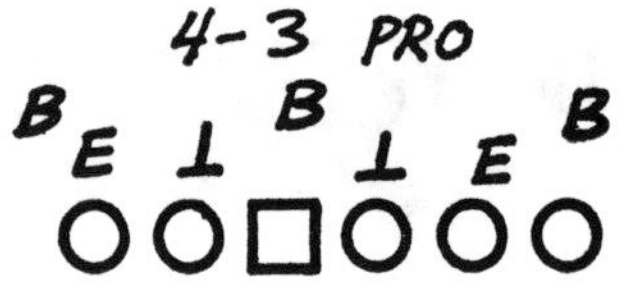

B   B   B
E   ⊥   ⊥   E
O O □ O O O

4-3 PRO

B   B   B
 E ⊥   ⊥ E
O O □ O O O

Your quarterbacks may also see a 4-3 Stack.

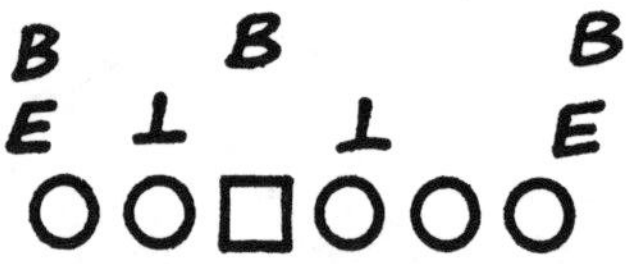

B   B   B
E   ⊥   ⊥   E
O O □ O O O

In addition, your quarterbacks might see a 4-3 College on one side and a 4-3 Pro on the other side.

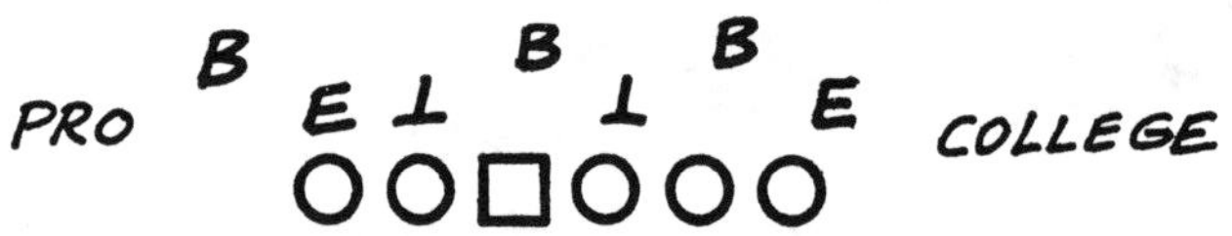

        B   B   B
PRO   E ⊥   ⊥   E   COLLEGE
      O O □ O O O

Or they might see a 4-3 Pro with a stack.

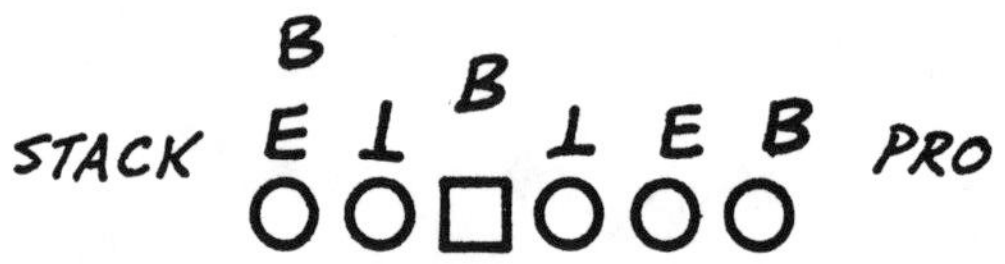

          B
          B   B
STACK   E ⊥   ⊥ E B   PRO
        O O □ O O O

After showing your quarterbacks the various kinds of 4-3 Defenses, show them the soft spots in those defenses. We use flash cards to illustrate the defenses and the soft spots. Here are the soft spots in the 4-3 College Defense.

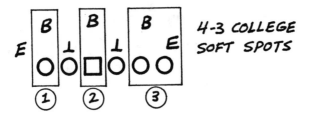

Here are the soft spots in the 4-3 Pro. The area circled is not as soft as the squared areas.

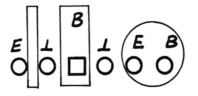

Here are the soft spots in the 4-3 Stack.

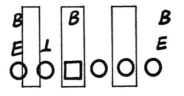

We then teach the plays we have selected to run against the 4-3 Defense. For example, in the first squared area with the 4-3 College, we like to run inside veer, isolation, and delay. In the second area, we prefer trap and windback. In the third squared area, we run isolation, outside veer, trap option, and 15-16 option (loaded option). Misdirection plays we use against the 4-3 Defense are the trap inside, delay, counter dive, windback, double dive, trap option and counter option.

Odd Front

People today call the Odd Front a 5-2. In professional football it is called a 3-4. Both are seven-man fronts with seven defenders close to the line of scrimmage.

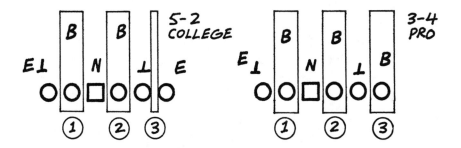

In the first area, we prefer to run inside veer. In the second or middle area, we want to run the isolation, power, counter dive, or fullback trap. In the tight end area, we want to run outside veer, 15-16 (loaded option) or trap option.

SPLIT DEFENSE

The Split Defense is an eight-man front. Our first rule is that we won't allow it. We will reduce the front.

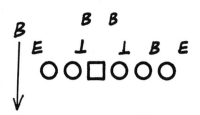

There are many different defensive adjustments that can be made in the Split Defense. One adjustment is the inside switch.

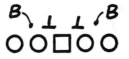

Another adjustment is the outside switch.

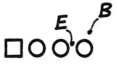

DANGER STUNTS

There are also what we call Danger Stunts. You must be able to block these stunts. If you work on them, they are easy to block. If you don't work on them, they are very difficult.

The Dog Stunt is with the defenders in the gaps. If one defender stunts, we call it a One-Dog Stunt. If all the defenders go, we call it a Two-Dog Stunt.

The Two-Dog Stunt:

The Twist Stunt is with the defensive tackles and linebackers.

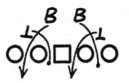

After showing our players the various adjustments in the Split Defense, we show them the soft spots in the defense.

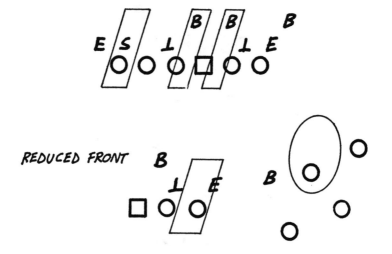

SPLIT DEFENSE RULES

First, reduce the front. Second, run to the reduced front. If the defense does not reduce the front, throw the ball until the defense is forced to reduce the front.

There are several ways to reduce the front. You can use a wide slot. We like to throw the "one" route or the "double-two" route until the front is reduced.

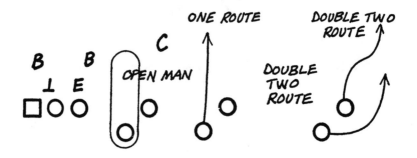

If the front is still not reduced and the defense is using Man Coverage, run post and cross patterns in the middle.

The non-reduced front with Man Coverage:

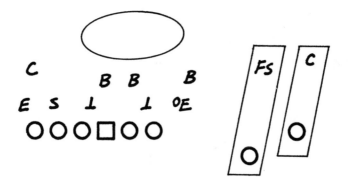

There are four effective patterns to use against the non-reduced front with Man Coverage.

The first pattern is a split end post. The slot back runs a Swing or Cross Pattern.

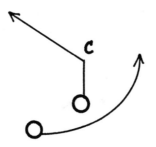

The second pattern is a tight end post. The tight end will be one-on-one with the cornerback.

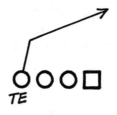

The third pattern is a 12 route thrown to the back in the middle.

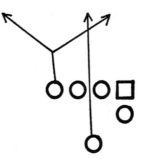

The fourth pattern is a slot back post.
Diagram:

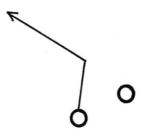

The front may also be reduced by motion.

FRONT REDUCED

Once the front is reduced, run power, inside option, isolation, or delay to the reduced front. Find out where the mismatch is in the front. Our number one play in this situation is the inside option.

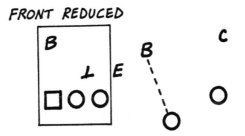

UNBALANCED DEFENSES

Unbalanced defenses will have more players to one side of the front than the other side. Against a 4-3 Offset Gap, we will run inside option to the "three" man side.

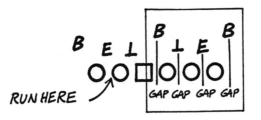

Against a 4-3 Offset Stack, we will run option away.

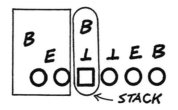

Against a 50 Offset Gap we will run option or isolation.

Against a 50 Stack, run option to the "three" defender side.

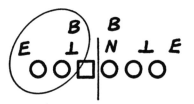

In college football today, instead of a true Odd Front, you will often see a 50 Eagle Reduced. First, we will run to the Eagle. If that is not successful, we will run to the Okie side.

If the defense is an Eagle Stack, we will run option to the Eagle Stack.

50 TACKLE

When the defensive tackle is head up on the tackle, we call him an Okie Tackle. When he is head up on the guard, we call him an Eagle Tackle. When the tackle is in the gap between the offensive guard and offensive tackle by himself, we call him a Slant Tackle.

GOAL-LINE AND SHORT-YARDAGE DEFENSES

Ninety to 95 percent of the time, most defenses still use Man Coverage in goal-line and short-yardage situations. Defenses put eight men to the front and try to get gap control and penetration. The defense wants to make something happen.

There are three main short-yardage and goal-line defenses.

EVEN PRO DEFENSE

The Even Pro Defense used to be the most common goal-line defense. It is not anymore.

To attack the Even Pro Defense, use a wide slot formation. Then run outside veer.

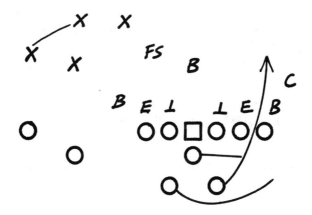

There are also other ways to attack the Even Pro Defense. You can block the end and run loaded option if you have a good running quarterback.

You can run inside veer away from the free safety on a direction call.

You can trap inside at the middle linebacker.

Your tight end can slow block for two seconds and then release. Throw to the tight end if the corner comes up. If the corner is back, run option.

If you have a good fullback, you can run a lot of power.

You can also trap inside or run Power "I."

6-5 STACK

The second type of common goal-line and short-yardage defense is the 6-5 Stack. Here, the defense is trying to outnumber the offense. The defense will look to blitz.

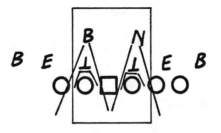

To attack the 6-5 Stack, run outside veer.

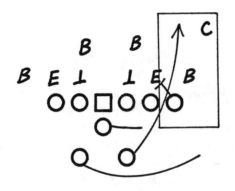

We will never run inside veer against a 6-5 Stack to the tight end side. In addition to outside veer, you can attack the 6-5 Stack with loaded option or lead option.

If the free safety moves, run inside option—probably from the "I" formation. There will be a three-on-two situation if the free safety moves over.

You can also run isolation.

6-5 WIDE

The 6-5 Wide is the goal-line defense we use most of the time. We will try to trap against the 6-5 Wide. If the linebackers are wide, try to seal them. We will run 32 trap. Otherwise, the game plan is the same as against a Stack.

ONE-BACK OFFENSE

If the defense is more physical, you may have to use a one-back offense in goal-line and short-yardage situations. You can then run power, windback, or trap.

If the defense stays with two linebackers, try to widen out the alley. Run your slot back in motion and use lead option pass or run. You will have two receivers and the quarterback running the ball as options to attack the widened alley.

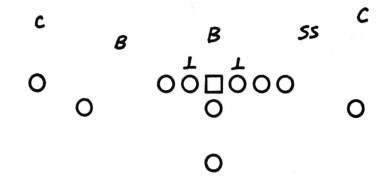

THE OPTION

There are several ways to attack in goal-line and short-yardage situations. In the opinion of our coaching staff, the best play on the goal line is the option.

AUTOMATIC SYSTEM

We believe that if you can run a good automatic system against your own defense and be successful, you have a good system. After all, your defense sees your offense every day.

We audible in three ways—the Color System, the Direction Call System, and the Check With Me System.

COLOR SYSTEM

We will have a true color for the week. This color could be changed at the half. If we call "Purple 24," we are running isolation. If we call "Purple 81," it is a slant pass to the 80 man (split end).

DIRECTION CALL SYSTEM

Our direction call system means a number. Plays are packaged in the huddle. Color means nothing here. The number after the color means everything.

For example, if "23, 24 isolation" is the call in the huddle, we will run 24 on any even number. If "Purple two" is called at the line of scrimmage, we will be running 24 isolation. If the call is "Purple three" at the line of scrimmage, we will run 23 isolation.

You can package two different plays with direction call. For example, "Option at 5" is outside veer and "Option at 4" is inside veer. Any even number is inside veer and any odd number is outside veer.

CHECK WITH ME

The quarterback goes in the huddle and gives the formation and count. He then comes out of the huddle. Any number the quarterback calls at the line of scrimmage is the true play. The color means nothing.

TWO OF THREE

In the first half, we will always use two of the three kinds of audibles. But before they can give the audible, our quarterbacks must understand the soft spots of the various defenses. They do not want to throw into the strength of the defense.

If the defense is balanced all the way across, they should run to the mismatch. If the defense is unbalanced, we want our quarterbacks to run away from the strength. We do not want them to throw into three-on-two coverage.

CHANGE THE CALL

If a direction call is called in the huddle, there may be a need to change the play. The true color will change the direction call—for example "24, 23 Purple three." The true color is given after the direction call.

SHORT LIST

The lower the classification of football, the shorter the list should be. For example, in junior high school, you may have one play on your short list. In high school, maybe three or four plays. In college, you might be up to eight or nine plays if you have an experienced quarterback. If your college quarterback is inexperienced, keep the short list at three or four plays.

We want three short-list running plays and three short-list passing plays. Our philosophy is that if we are having trouble with our automatic system, we will subtract from our short list. We don't want confusion. The more experienced our quarterback, the longer the short list can be.

You must make sure your short list is designated toward your opponent's weaknesses on defense. Don't just have a list to have a list. Your list might have to be adjusted during the game.

Our philosophy is that it is not enough for the quarterbacks to know the short list. The first twenty-two players on offense should know the short list and how to execute it in terms of assignments. We have a daily time for audibles in practice. We also test our players with written examinations. They must know the fronts, coverages, and short-list audibles before they play in the game on Saturday.

A good audible system and a good knowledgeable short list could be the difference between winning and losing—not only games but also championships. Again, that short list must be aimed at your opponent's weaknesses.

You must show your team the reason for your automatic system. This will develop confidence in your system. The athlete today wants to know *why* something is being done and you as a coach should have a reason.

SPEND TIME

It takes longer to teach an inexperienced quarterback. Naturally, he will make some mistakes. But you want him making those mistakes in practice, not in the game.

In our system, the more experienced the quarterback, the more he thinks and acts like the coaching staff.

If you believe in something, you must spend time on it. The more repetitions, the better the development of a conditioned reflex to a certain situation.

AUDIBLE RULES

Our first rule is that when in doubt, give the ball to your best back and run to your best blockers. In the passing game, when in doubt, throw to your most reliable receiver.

Our second rule is that if the quarterback audibles, he should have a reason for doing so.

If the quarterback has been taught to audible and doesn't, we first look at how we are teaching. If it is not a teaching problem, the quarterback may need to spend more time on film study.

FIELD AREAS

We make defensive files on every team we play. We then try to show our quarterbacks what to expect in different situations from different areas of the field.

We say the area from zero to ten yards out is a very critical area. In this area, we will try to do what we do best.

From the ten-yard line to the twenty-five is another critical area. From one twenty-five-yard line to the other, we will take what the defense gives us. From the twenty-five-yard line in is another critical area. From the twenty-yard line to the ten is generally three-down area. If we don't get the first down, we generally kick the field goal. From the ten-yard line to the goal line is four-down area unless we have suffered substantial losses on one or both of the first two plays.

WASTE DOWNS

On second-and-short in the three-down area or third-and-short in the four-down area, we may go for paydirt.

KNOWING THE GAME PLAN

In the 1950s and 1960s, most quarterbacks did not know the game plan. Today, they must know the game plan if they are to be as effective as possible. This is true of both college and high school quarterbacks. By knowing the game plan, your quarterbacks will feel more secure. They will have more confidence in you as a coach and in the game plan you have prepared.

GRADING YOUR QUARTERBACKS

The more knowledge your quarterbacks have, the better your team will be. Grade your quarterbacks on technique, but also grade them on reading defenses and how they audible.

11

IMPLEMENTING AN
EFFECTIVE TEAM
OFFENSE

We believe in the option package, the quick-passing game, the sprint-out passing game, and the play-action pass. We also believe in the misdirection game and the trap inside.

Against a balanced front, it is very important to find the mismatch. If the front is unbalanced, run away from the strength of the defense. If the secondary is unbalanced, it is very important to run away from the unbalanced secondary. If the front is unbalanced and the secondary is unbalanced, attack the unbalanced secondary or try to control it with motion.

If the defense is in an eight-man front, reduce the front to at least seven. If your quarterbacks are seeing many coverages in their pre-snap read, run motion to get a pre-snap read.

In option football, you must open up the alleys with either the option—the quick-passing game or with motion. If you are having trouble with pursuit or sealing the inside to get outside, run misdirection, traps, or the option to get to the alleys.

To implement an effective team offense, run many different formations. If something is working, stay with it until the defense takes it away.

Every year you will have different personnel. Take advantage of that personnel. In the off season, try to project how many times you want your fullbacks to carry the ball. Also do this with the quarterback and running-back position. Project how many times you want to throw the ball and out of which formations. Try to figure out how to get the ball to your best receivers and try to anticipate how defenses will try to take this away. You must also have a good plan of attack against Nickel Defenses.

TEAM OFFENSIVE DRILLS

You must have realistic drills that you can associate with game (11-on-11) situations. *A drill is useless unless it is realistic to game activity.*

GET-OFF DRILL

A team that gets a lot of offsides penalties is a team that does not practice enough on get-off drills. Our goal in every game is not to have more than one offsides and one backfield in motion penalty. Through the years, we have had more trouble with backfield in motion penalties than offsides. At times, we have gotten off the ball so quickly the officials have thought we were leaving before the snap of the ball.

If you are an option team, you will usually win if you get off quicker at the line of scrimmage. We teach "get off" for ten minutes every practice. We also audible in our get-off drills. The more repetitions, the more the improvement.

We want our coaches coaching on every play. For example, our offensive line coach is situated next to the line so he can see how our linemen are coming off the ball. Our offensive line coach also makes sure that calls are being made at the line of scrimmage. As we have mentioned, our blocking system centers around guard-tackle calls which must be given on every play.

Our receiver coach makes sure our receivers come off the

same whether the play is a run or a pass. We don't want our receivers loafing when the play is a run.

The quarterback coach is looking for technique on every play. He makes sure that the quarterback is set for one second and that the quarterback doesn't give away the direction of the play. We always want our quarterbacks looking from right to left when giving signals so they don't tip off the play.

The quarterback coach is also looking for the "third hand" in our quarterbacks' technique. This means he is making sure the quarterback brings the ball back into his stomach when taking the snap. This is a must in preventing fumbles on the exchange.

The backfield coach is stationed so he can see how quickly our fullback and running back are getting off the ball. He is also checking to see that our backs are running the correct patch. For example, on the option, we would like the back to run through the outside hip of the guard instead of the inside hip.

Diagram of Get-Off Drill:

Our players do get-off correctly or they run hills. This is a discipline point. We feel we are not punishing them but we are reminding them of what it takes to win.

HALF LINE

To us, half line is a good, realistic drill. We try to show the strong side and the quick or open side all the defensive looks they will see in a game. You can either hit or polish in half line. You are teaching the ability to block at the point of attack.

Here are some strongside looks we can expect.

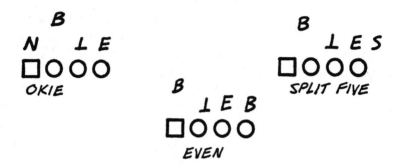

Here are some examples of quickside looks.

SIX-ON-SIX DRILL

It is important to cut people off. You can't do this in half line but you can in six-on-six. We are always talking about cutting off pursuit. If you "seam it" right, you can get the big play.

FIVE-ON-FIVE INSIDE DRILL

This drill teaches how to attack in the middle of the defense. You can't run to the perimeter all the time. You must also make the defense stay at home.

In five-on-five, we run trap and power or our inside game. Here we will run trap and power.

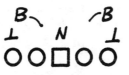

Here, we will run our inside game.

$$B$$

$$E \quad \perp \quad \perp \quad E$$

$$\bigcirc \bigcirc \square \bigcirc \bigcirc$$

THREE-ON-THREE DRILL

This drill teaches blocking and tackling. It also teaches the backs to hit up and make yardage after the first hit.

The defense is seeking to defeat the blocker, get to the ball carrier and tackle him. These are basic fundamentals. Football is getting very sophisticated. Still, 95 percent of the time, the team that blocks and tackles the best wins.

We do the three-on-three drill once a week. Since there are few players involved, the drill does cut down on injuries. But, it still teaches fundamentals.

SEVEN-ON-SEVEN PERIMETER DRILL

This drill is live. The offense can run option, lead option-quick passing game, sprint out, or play action. We usually do the seven-on-seven drill once a week.

The drill is realistic in that it teaches the receivers to block and catch the ball with contact. It also teaches the defensive backs to come up and play the run. It teaches backs to get yardage in the one-on-one situation after the first hit. It teaches quarterbacks different coverages. The quarterbacks can also audible.

Seven-on-seven is live except for the quarterback. The quarterback doesn't get a true look at getting hit. We don't like this, but we have to live with it.

The quarterback runs our game plan for Saturday's game. We can see how well he runs the game plan and correct the things he is doing incorrectly.

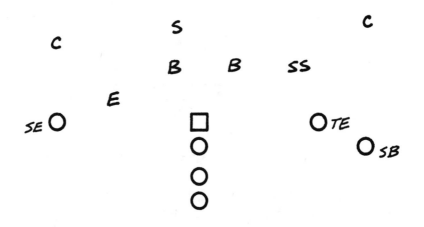

SKELETON DRILL

The same people are involved as in the seven-on-seven perimeter drill. However, this is a throwing-only drill with the offensive line pass blocking.

We put in anticipated coverages and try to attack them. We throw fifteen to twenty minutes. Everything is charted—passes attempted, passes completed, passes intercepted, dropped passes, total yardage, and total yardage per pass. To us, any gain over twenty yards is a big play and any gain over thirty yards is an exceptionally big play.

We try to teach our players what we think is necessary to win. For example, in a ten-game schedule, we consider throwing ten interceptions good and five exceptional. Our goal is no turnovers for touchdowns during the season.

As an option team, we want to complete 54 percent of our passes. If you are predominately a passing team, we believe you are going to have to complete more than 54 percent of your passes to win.

12

DEVELOPING THE WINNING EDGE

You must develop your team physically, mentally, and emotionally to have and maintain the winning edge.

PHYSICAL DEVELOPMENT

To win, you must execute, and to execute, you need physical development. Our players develop physically through a weight program, a quickness program, a stretching program, and a conditioning program. We have summer, winter and spring programs.

WEIGHT PROGRAM

Our weight program is designed to develop strength in all of our players and bulk (weight gain) in some. A weight program develops confidence in a player and may also intimidate an opponent.

We have a reward system for our players. To reward players, we must first test them. Because of time factors, we use only two tests. We use the bench press to test upper body strength and the squat to test the lower body. The minimum a player must be able to bench press to join our Bench Press Club is 300 pounds. The minimum he must be able to squat is 400 pounds.

We test every one and one-half to two months. We give away a small plaque to the leader of each of the two lifts. Members of the Bench Press and Squat Clubs get T-shirts.

QUICKNESS PROGRAM

If you have quick feet, you will react quickly. There are ten stations for our quickness program, including jumping benches and jumping rope.

STRETCHING PROGRAM

A stretching program will help a player's speed and flexibility. Since we have implemented a stretching program, the number of pulled muscles on our team has been greatly reduced.

CONDITIONING PROGRAM

To be perfectly honest, our players do not like this program as well as the others. But you cannot create the winning edge without it. Our conditioning program lasts fifteen to seventeen minutes—about the length of the fourth quarter. The program includes ups and downs (grass drill), running hills, and 40-yard dashes that have to be run in a certain time. These are only some examples of our conditioning program.

We are constantly telling our players why they are doing things in the conditioning program. They must have the ability to reach down and push themselves. Many times you have heard or said that "one team really wanted it more." We believe this can be taught.

MENTAL DEVELOPMENT

Mental development is also a big part of the winning edge. For example, you must have positive thinking. You must believe you can. Positive thinking brings about positive results. Negative thinking brings about negative results (mind over matter).

GAME PLAN

In the execution of the game plan, we do not want to beat ourselves with mental mistakes. Games are lost because of one mental mistake. We might accept a physical mistake but we will never accept a mental mistake.

Our offensive game plan includes a running game plan and a passing game plan. We gear our offensive game plan to what we feel are weaknesses in our opponent's personnel and philosophy.

We try to attack the soft spots in our opponent's defense and see how we can create mismatches. Our philosophy is to try to break down our opponent's defensive mental tendencies. Our opponents know we have certain offensive tendencies. We want to have a plan to break down that tendency chart. To do this, we must scout ourselves and know our own tendencies.

THREE FIELD AREAS

Our offensive game plan is especially related to three areas of the field. These are critical areas.

Critical area number one is coming out—from our own one-yard line to our own twenty-yard line. We devise our strategy based on what we do best and what we think we can do to create a mismatch.

Critical area number two is from our own twenty- to forty-yard lines. It is crucial to move the ball in this area to get field position.

Critical area number three is from our opponent's twenty-five-yard line to the goal line. We have a 3.4-yards-per-play philosophy in the three-down area and a 2.5-yards-per-play philosophy in the four-down area. On first down from the ten-yard line, we will probably be using a 2.5 philosophy.

In game plan, we make out plays to be run from these critical areas of the field. We have first-down-and-ten plays for the critical areas. We do the same thing for second-and-short, second-and-medium, and second-and-long situations from the critical areas. We also make out plays for third-and-short, third-and-medium, and third-and-long situations. In addition, we make out plays for fourth-and-short and fourth-and-medium situations. On fourth-and-long, we will usually kick the field goal.

HASH-MARK GAME PLAN

We also have a hash-mark game plan. For example, maybe we will run to the wide side of the field. If the defense is covering the wide side, maybe we will plan to run away.

TOUGH-CALL LIST

Our tough-call list is for times when we really have to make certain yardage. The list is usually five or six plays. It might vary according to what is going for us in the game. Again, the list is based on our personnel and strengths. It is also based on our opponent's weaknesses, either by personnel or by philosophy.

AUTOMATIC SHORT LIST

This part of our game plan has been discussed in Chapter X, "Training the Option Quarterback."

SPECIAL PLAYS

If we cannot line up physically with our opponent, we will run a lot of different formations and special plays. We call these plays Momentum Changers or Big Plays. Sometimes they can be used effectively after a turnover when the defense is a little disorganized. If we go into a game with superior manpower, we probably won't run many special plays. If we are the underdog or the game is even, we will take more chances. We will gamble and hope it works out. Remember, if it doesn't work, a special play could be a Momentum Changer for your opponent.

DOUBLE PASS

This special play can be run out of play action or sprint out. On sprint out, the quarterback takes five steps. The tight end slow blocks for three seconds because most teams read it for two seconds. The tight end must be disciplined and not get out of there too fast.

The receiver takes two steps back inside and goes to the original tight end area—but behind the line of scrimmage. The quarterback "looks it off" downfield and then throws backwards to the receiver. If the pass is fumbled, the ball is live.

For the play to be successful, you must get the cornerback over to read and come up.

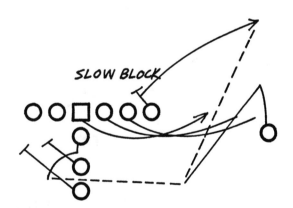

HALFBACK PASS

The back runs to the corner to make the play look like a run. Sometimes we pull the guard. The halfback pass can also be run off quick-pitch action, sweep action, or option action.

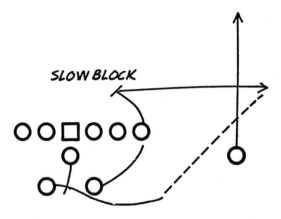

THROWBACK PASS TO THE QUARTERBACK

This can be an effective play if your quarterback is a good athlete and has the ability to run with the ball after he catches it.

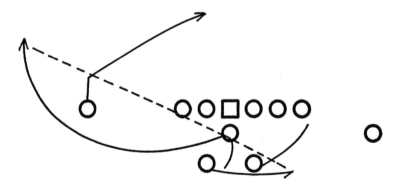

WIDE RECEIVER SCREEN

We usually run our wide receiver screens off option action. It helps to have a receiver who can run like a running back and can break tackles after he catches the ball.

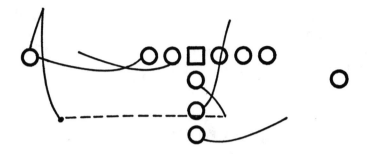

NO-HUDDLE OFFENSE

The No-Huddle Offense can be a big Momentum Changer. There are two main reasons to use it. First, it is a surprise. Second, you can force a multiple defensive team to one defense.

You need a quarterback with good composure. The No-Huddle Offense has not been too difficult for us to execute because we use the automatic short list and two-minute offense all the time. If we didn't, it would be a big adjustment.

SOME GAME PLAN REMINDERS

There are a lot of lists in our game plan, but there is also a lot of repetition in those plays and in those lists. We are still trying to keep the KISS (Keep It Simple Stupid) philosophy.

Also, do not forget how you got there. If something is working well, stay with it until the defense adjusts and stops it. For example, if the defense is covering the field, run away to the hash mark. Try to get a one-on-one or two-on-two situation in the passing game and eliminate the three-on-two by formation or by motion. If the defense is Zone Under, throw the ball in the open spots deep. If the defense is Zone on Top and Man Under, throw in the short zones.

Attack what the defense is giving you and attack the mismatch. If you attack the defensive strength, you are going to get beaten.

Finally, you can have the greatest game plan in the world but your players must execute it if you are going to win. Don't just be a chalkboard coach. Devise your game plan within the philosophy of what you believe in and what you can teach in a one-week period.

GAME PLAN TESTS

Again, repetition is the key. The more you go over your game plan with chalk talks, films, and tests, the better your players will understand it. This will build your player's confidence and give them a positive attitude toward the game plan.

GAME ADJUSTMENTS

To win, you have to be able to adjust during the game and at the half. The head coach has a copy of our opponent's anticipated defenses and tendencies. The coaches in the press box also have a copy. By the half, or even in the middle of the second quarter, we would like to have some tendencies established as to what the defense is doing against our formations, motion, etc.

At the half, everything is timed and organized carefully. The defense goes to one part of the locker room and the offense to another. There is something available to the players for quick energy.

The head coach talks to the defensive coaches first and then to the offensive coaches. If the opponent is beating us with the run or the pass or stopping us, we want to know *why*. For example, if the opponent is running off tackle effectively to the tight end side and we cannot stop it with a balanced front, we may have to go unbalanced or begin stunting.

After the head coach talks to both units, there is a period where the position coaches can talk with their personnel. Finally, the head coach talks to the team as a whole.

You will very seldom find our coaching staff shouting at the players during the halftime. We believe the half is a time to make adjustments and to offer encouragement. If you are shouting, you are probably not making any adjustments.

We don't generally shout after the game either. If we are unsatisfied, we will talk to the players Sunday night after we have had a chance to look at the films.

WEATHER ADJUSTMENTS

You must be prepared to play in snow, rain, cold, wind, or extreme heat. Try to have an idea of what the weather will be like on game day. It is important that you convince your players they can play effectively in any kind of weather.

Your players may have to bring two or three different pairs of shoes to a game and find out which will be the most effective. You may also have to consider a change of uniforms at the half under certain conditions.

THEORY OF TIME-OUTS

Do you want to save your time-outs for the end of the quarter or the end of the game or do you want to use them as situations arise? If you have a Big Play situation early in the game that might be a Momentum Changer, do you want to use a time-out?

You must also decide whether to use your time-outs on offense or defense or a mixture of the two.

Our philosophy is to try to control the game's momentum. We want to make sure we keep moving the ball. Therefore, we will take a time-out on offense as the situation arises. If we are down three touchdowns and have three time-outs left late in the game, those three time-outs probably aren't going to do us much good.

One thing that can save time-outs is being organized in the Ready Area. We have one coach responsible for the Ready Area. He must have any player or group of players waiting in the Ready Area *well before* they are to enter the game. For example, if we have forced the offense into a passing situation, he will have our Nickel back waiting and ready to go.

MENTAL TOUGHNESS

We talk a lot about self-discipline and mental toughness. We believe that physical fatigue is caused more by a lack of mental toughness than by physical strain. But, this has to be taught.

We believe that the team with the most mental toughness will win in the kicking game. Players have a tendency to ease up when covering punts and kickoffs. In a close game, the team that wins the kicking game usually wins the game.

Mental toughness also has a great deal to do with momentum. For example, from the twenty-five-yard line in, we want seven points—not three. If the defense stops us, it is a Momentum Changer.

If we block a kick, it is a Momentum Changer. The same thing happens if the opponent blocks one of our kicks.

A team must think it can find a way to win. We tell our players the game is divided into offense, defense, the kicking game, and turnovers. If we can win the turnovers and two of the other three, we believe we can win the game. Execution is the key here and it must be thought about.

We also talk to our players about dedication to a cause or ultimate goal. We tell our players we can beat our opponents if we out-work them, if we out-technique them, and if we beat them in the fourth quarter.

EMOTIONAL DEVELOPMENT

A team can be physically and mentally prepared but it won't reach its fullest potential unless it is emotionally prepared as well.

How emotional should a team be? There are many ways to skin a cat. The head coach at Carroll College is an emotional person and his teams reflect his personality. They are very emotional.

INTENSITY LEVEL

We believe you can prepare your team to an average intensity level each game. We also believe you can prepare your team to a very *high point* emotionally once during the regular season.

Some coaches play a team they think they can beat at homecoming to keep the alumni happy. In filling out our schedule, we pick out the team we really want to beat as our homecoming opponent. Since I have been at Carroll, we have lost only one homecoming game. We have beaten a lot of teams we probably couldn't have beaten if we hadn't been emotionally "sky high" to win for the players' fathers, the seniors, etc.

The problem with getting to a *high point* emotionally can be the next week. Preparation can be difficult when your team comes back down to earth after being so "sky high." We attempt to do things in practice the next week that will bring the team back emotionally.

PRE-GAME TALK

The head coach talks to the team before every game. The pre-game talk lasts fifteen to twenty minutes and can take up to an hour to prepare. The subject matter is limited to no more than three topics.

In most cases, the pre-game talk is designed to bring the team to an average intensity level. A team with an average intensity level will do a good job of concentrating and eliminating mental mistakes. A lackadaisical team will make mental mistakes.

We may also bring in outsiders to say a few words or one of the assistant coaches might speak. But the head coach will always give a pre-game talk.

PRIDE

We talk a lot about team pride. We talk about the "Two Hs"—Hit and Hustle. We talk about the "Two Big Cs"—Confidence and Courage. We talk about the "Big H"—Honesty to your self. We tell our players that if they can look in the mirror daily and say they are doing the best they can, they are on the right track.

We always talk about 110 percent effort. We want our players to give 110 percent effort, to show courage, and to be honest.

SIGNS

We still believe in signs in the locker room though some people think we are old-fashioned. We have signs all over pertaining to our next opponent and to our own character.

TRADITION

We try to maintain a winning tradition and must continually work to do this. Five years of effort to gain a winning tradition can be lost in one year.

UNITY

We emphasize unity and togetherness. Football is a team game. If ten players do their jobs on a play and one doesn't, that play could result in a loss. Our players hold hands in the huddle to emphasize this notion of unity.

CAPTAINS

We are point-blank honest with our players. We tell them we can't do it by ourselves. Our captains have to be an enforcement within.

Our captains are elected by their peers. We meet with the captains twice a week during the season and expect them to call a team meeting once a week.

Our captains are given a list of the things it takes to be a good captain. The list includes:

1. Emotional leadership
2. Leadership by playing the game with *great desire*
3. Leadership by doing a great job 110 percent of the time
4. Leadership by example on and off the field

5. Outstanding will to win
6. First on the field
7. Last off the field
8. Getting everybody *ready* when things are going bad
9. Calling team meetings and telling the team we are all in it to win and be together. *We must work hard to win*
10. Playing with little hurts
11. Helping the younger players to be true "Saints"
12. Being on *top* or near the *top* in the statistics
13. Being *loyal* to the coaching staff and to the team
14. *Stop, stop* the crybabies
15. Giving everything in your body and mind for the "Fighting Saints"

SENIORS

To have a good nucleus of seniors is an advantage. Most seniors realize that it is the last time around and they want to make it a good one. If you don't have a lot of senior leadership, you are going to need a lot of leadership within.

13

BUILDING THE OFFENSE IS A YEAR-ROUND JOB

It is not enough to put in an offense in pre-fall practice. You must plan and organize your offense year round to stay ahead of your opponents' defensive adjustments.

POST-SEASON PREPARATION

We start preparing our offense for the next season as soon as our last game is over. We take into consideration our main plays, formations, and personnel from the just-completed season.

EVALUATING OUR PLAYS

We know how many times we have run a play during the season because we keep weekly reports. We figure out how many yards that play averaged during the season. We also look at the defenses used against the play, our blocking schemes and down selections, and the area of the field from which the play was run.

From this information, we come up with a philosophy on the play for the next season. We consider what personnel we have returning. We also consider what adjustments we need to make on the play. If the play has been successful, we try to anticipate defensive changes against it.

We make out a final *temporary* conclusion about what we are going to do with the play. This will be readjusted in the spring.

Some plays may have had a limited success ratio during the season. We try to find out *why*. Is it because of our teaching of technique, our philosophy, our personnel, or our opponents' defensive adjustments?

A decision is then made on whether to continue using the play the following season, eliminate it, or add a new wrinkle or blocking scheme to it. If we decide to add a new wrinkle or blocking scheme, it will be tried out in the spring.

Every play we have is analyzed in such a manner. We keep in mind the defensive fronts, stunts, and secondary coverages we will see.

A list is made of successful plays from the past season. A list is also made of unsuccessful plays and the reasons why those plays were unsuccessful. We study the plays that didn't work in more depth than the plays that did work.

EVALUATION OF THE COACHING STAFF

We rate ourselves as a coaching staff with respect to technique and philosophy. We also rate our game plan and procedure. Did we have a sound game plan? Did we stay with our game plan or did we panic? When we had to get away from our game plan, did we have a good adjustment plan?

EVALUATION OF PERSONNEL

In evaluating personnel, we list each player's strengths and weaknesses from a technique standpoint, a physical standpoint, a quickness and agility standpoint, and an attitude standpoint.

After a player reads the report, he is free to add his own comments. The player is then given a winter, spring, summer program. This program is designed to decrease his limitations and increase his strengths.

RECRUITING

Being a college team, we can recruit. But before we can recruit, we have to know what we need. We have a temporary plan of what we want to do offensively to fill that recruiting list.

The plan includes: 1. The main plays that we will build our offense around in the upcoming season. 2. The main formations we will use in the upcoming season. 3. The types of motion we plan to concentrate on. 4. The things we can do to improve the offense with the talent available. 5. We try to figure out what defenses did last season that they hadn't done in previous seasons against us and *why*. If those new defensive wrinkles were successful, we try to come up with a temporary plan against them. 6. We also try to figure out our opponents' defensive plans for the next season. Will they be the same? Will they be different? If we know an opponent is making defensive changes but don't know what they are, we will try to find out. With that in mind, our opponents' spring games are scouted.

SPRING FOOTBALL

In January, we start making a definite plan of the things we are going to coach in spring ball. We always cover pass technique and review coaching points. We also cover new technique and coaching points. In addition, we may be covering experimental technique where we try to implement something new.

Philosophy is also a big part of our spring-ball planning. To us, philosophy is important because it gives direction. Those who don't have a philosophy are the ones who panic in a given situation. This is not to say that we as a coaching staff have never panicked. We have. However, we are constantly trying to better ourselves in this area. Having a philosophy will increase stability and minimize panic.

We usually find out we have too much offense in during spring ball. We can't execute everything the way we want to.

When spring ball is over, we make a final conclusion on what we want to keep and what we want to do away with. We figure out what we are going to make a commitment to. After spring ball, we will not make any changes in our philosophy and plays except for special plays and motion. If we lose with the commitment we have made, we lose with it. If we win with it, it motivates us for next year to come up with another good plan.

FILM STUDY

How many times is enough to watch a game film? Our rule is that you have completed the necessary time in film study when you have an almost photographic memory of what the film contains. For example, you should know what the first play on the film is. You should also know the second play and right on down the line. When you can do that, you have probably watched the film enough.

Films are a valuable check on both coaches and players. Our coaches and players are told that "the film doesn't lie."

Films give mental discipline and humility to a coaching staff. There are many game films our staff would like to throw away and erase from our minds. Many times we have watched films and wondered how we could make so many mistakes, whether it be in game plan, play selection, improper fundamentals of players, or other matters.

In addition to checking ourselves, films are a valuable tool for scouting our opponents.

CLINICS, SPRING BALL AT OTHER CAMPUSES, AND PROFESSIONAL CAMPS

As a staff, we try to attend two clinics a year. We always go to a college campus to observe a week of its spring football program.

We also try to visit a professional camp early in July. We want to know what *they* are doing in certain situations. We want to know what they are doing in such areas as philosophy and teaching. We make a list of new ideas or drills that can help our program.

BOOKS AND ARTICLES

Like most coaching staffs, we try to keep abreast of the latest articles and books pertaining to football technique and philosophy. Do not overlook any source of printed material that may help your program.

IN CONCLUSION

We always check our accomplishments and liabilities pertaining to the previous season. We spend more time on our shortcomings than we do on our accomplishments.

We believe that coaching *does* make a difference. We believe organization *does* make a difference. We believe planning year round *does* make a difference. We believe having a philosophy *does* make a difference.

Building the offense is a year-round commitment. We believe that commitment and direction will lead to a positive outcome.

This book has discussed our philosophy and how we teach the offense. The option package offense works—with players of varying degrees of talent and against many different defensive packages and personnel. The option package has worked for us. It can also work for you.

INDEX